THE HUMAN LOAD

Why Modern Life Feels Heavier Than It Should

Dwayne Walter

THE HUMAN LOAD
Why Modern Life Feels Heavier Than It Should

ISBN 978-150-915-77-7 PBK
ISBN 978-1506-915-71-5 EBK

March 2026

Published and Distributed by
First Edition Design Publishing, Inc.
P.O. Box 17646, Sarasota, FL 34276-3217
www.firsteditiondesignpublishing.com

To Anwei, my wife—
whose presence, insight, and quiet strength
became the deepest inspiration for this work.

Table of Contents

INTRODUCTION

The Weight We Don't Know How to Name

Something feels heavier about modern life, even for people who are doing well. This heaviness is not confined to the anxious or the unlucky. It appears among the educated, the materially secure, the technologically fluent, and the outwardly successful. People report feeling stretched, restless, and perpetually behind, even when no single crisis explains the sensation. They sleep, but do not feel rested. They are informed, but not oriented. They are connected, but often feel alone with their thoughts. The discomfort is real, yet difficult to describe without sounding either ungrateful or melodramatic.

We have names for pieces of this experience. We talk about stress, burnout, anxiety, overload, distraction, and depression. These terms are not wrong, but they are incomplete. They describe symptoms more than causes. They medicalize what is often structural, and they individualize what is frequently environmental. They imply that something is wrong with the person, when something may be misaligned in the world the person is trying to inhabit.

This book proposes a different name for the condition: **the human load**. By "load," I do not mean hardship in the traditional sense. I do not mean poverty, violence, or deprivation, though those still exist and matter deeply. I mean the cumulative cognitive, emotional, and attentional weight imposed by modern systems that never fully resolve, never fully switch off, and never fully stop asking for response. This load is not dramatic. It is persistent. It does not announce itself as danger. It announces itself as obligation.

Crucially, the human load is not the result of personal weakness. It is the predictable outcome of living inside environments that demand continuous vigilance, constant choice, and ongoing self-management. The nervous system did not evolve for inboxes without bottoms, identities without boundaries, or futures that must be continuously anticipated and optimized. Yet these are now normal conditions of life.

Part I of this book begins by stepping back in time. It examines the kinds of social worlds in which human psychology originally took shape—worlds that were bounded, rhythmical, and limited in informational bandwidth. These worlds were not idyllic, and they were often harsh, but they provided psychological structure that modern life quietly dissolves. Understanding this contrast is not an exercise in nostalgia. It is a way of seeing how much invisible scaffolding once supported mental equilibrium.

Part II turns to the core pressures that now define daily experience. It explores chronic stress not as drama, but as unfinished loops that keep the body in partial activation. It examines technological saturation as the moment when tools became environments, shaping attention rather than merely assisting it. It looks at choice, comparison, and identity labor as burdens that arrive disguised as freedom. Throughout, the focus remains structural. The goal is not to catalogue complaints, but to understand how modern systems produce predictable psychological costs.

Part III widens the lens further. It considers how measurement, surveillance, and evaluation—often introduced in the name of efficiency or fairness—alter inner life by creating a constant sense of exposure. It examines acceleration as a self-reinforcing dynamic that compresses time and erodes reflection. This section is less about technology itself than about the incentives it amplifies and the assumptions it quietly embeds about what humans can bear. Only after this diagnosis does the book turn toward orientation.

Part IV asks what modern technology *could* be doing for human beings, rather than what we fear it might do to us. It argues that the defining human capacity is not productivity, speed, or even intelligence in the narrow sense, but **sentience**: the ability to reflect, judge, assign meaning, and take responsibility within complex systems. From this perspective, automation and advanced technology need not threaten human worth. Properly aligned, they can reduce drudgery, protect civilization from collapse, and return human attention to the domains where it matters most.

This section also confronts a common fantasy: that the solution to modern weight lies in going back. It does not. Earlier worlds were smaller and sometimes psychologically lighter, but they were also more fragile, more exclusionary, and less capable of protecting human life at scale. Advanced civilization without advanced technology is not virtuous. It is vulnerable. The challenge is not to dismantle modern systems, but to civilize them—to design tools, institutions, and norms that respect human limits rather than testing them indefinitely.

The argument of this book is deliberately staged. It begins with diagnosis because orientation without diagnosis becomes wishful thinking. It ends with direction because diagnosis without direction becomes despair. Between the two lies a simple claim with demanding implications: if human awareness is finite and valuable, then civilization must be built to protect it.

The human load is real. It is structural. And it is not the final word. This book is an attempt to name the weight we have learned to carry silently—and to ask whether a future powerful enough to transform the world might also be wise enough to remain human.

PART I — BEFORE THE LOAD

CHAPTER 1

A Nervous System Designed for Intermittence

There is a peculiar kind of fatigue that does not come from hunger, illness, grief, or hard physical labor. It comes from days that are, on paper, normal. You wake, you function, you answer a few messages, you attend to errands, you solve small problems, you sit down to rest—and discover that rest does not quite arrive. Your body is not in crisis, yet it does not truly stand down. Your mind is not facing danger, yet it keeps scanning as if danger were simply hidden behind the next email, the next notification, the next obligation you have not yet remembered.

Modern people often call this stress. They are not wrong. But the word is too small. Stress suggests something sharp, episodic, and temporary—an event that visits, disrupts, and then leaves. What many of us experience instead is closer to a background condition: a low, persistent tension that never quite resolves. A subtle readiness. An inability to exhale fully. This is not merely "being busy." It is the feeling of living under a standing order: stay alert, stay available, stay prepared.

Human beings are not built for that kind of permanence.

The basic machinery of the human nervous system was shaped in worlds where stress arrived in bursts and ended decisively. For most of our history, the most consequential pressures were immediate and physical: predation, conflict, exposure, hunger, injury, childbirth, sudden weather, sudden violence. These were not romantic lives; they were often harsh. Yet they had a feature modern life increasingly lacks: **closure**. A threat appeared. The body surged into readiness. The threat passed—or it did not. Either way, the cycle ended. The organism returned to baseline, because baseline was not optional. It was the condition of survival.

In such a world, the stress response is a marvel. It mobilizes energy, narrows focus, sharpens reflexes, and temporarily deprioritizes everything not required for immediate action. The body becomes a problem-solving instrument. For a short time, it is designed to care about one thing and one thing only: getting through the moment.

The problem is not that modern life triggers this response. The problem is that modern life triggers it **without finishing the story**.

A predator either catches you or fails. An argument either ends or escalates. A storm either passes or breaks you. Modern stressors, by contrast, rarely conclude. They linger. They morph. They multiply. An email can be answered, but the underlying demand remains: more will come. A bill can be paid, but the system that produces bills remains. A task can be completed, but the culture of tasks does not end. Even a victory is seldom final; it becomes a new baseline, then a new expectation, then—quietly—another obligation.

The nervous system notices this. Not in words, but in posture. In sleep. In the subtle hum of vigilance that continues long after the day's "work" is technically done.

This is the first principle of the human load: **the body is prepared for intermittent strain, not continuous activation**. Modern life has turned many forms of strain into an ambient environment. It is not that we are always panicking. It is that we are rarely fully safe—not in reality, perhaps, but in the emotional logic of the organism. We live inside a condition of partial readiness: ready to respond, ready to update, ready to defend ourselves socially, ready to explain, ready to perform.

Even when we are alone.

One reason this heaviness is hard to name is that modern stress is frequently non-physical and non-lethal. It is often social, symbolic, and bureaucratic. The threats are not teeth and claws; they are reputational risk, financial uncertainty, professional evaluation, social exclusion, and the dread of falling behind in ways we cannot always specify. Many of these threats are not imaginary. They are real pressures that shape the trajectory of a life. But they operate in a strange register: the consequences may be significant, yet the body cannot complete the cycle through action. You cannot outrun an inbox. You cannot fight a metric. You cannot physically resolve a diffuse expectation.

So the system stays activated, waiting for the moment that never arrives.

This helps explain a modern paradox: people can feel exhausted even without obvious hardship. They are not suffering from one catastrophe; they are carrying dozens of micro-pressures that never fully discharge. Some are external. Some are self-imposed. Many are simply the price of living inside complex systems. The body experiences them as unfinished loops—open circuits. A mind that can't stop thinking is not necessarily a mind that loves thinking. It may be a mind that senses unresolved obligations and tries, endlessly, to locate the missing endpoint.

The effect is not just psychological. It seeps into the texture of everyday life. Sleep becomes lighter, more easily interrupted, as if the body is reluctant to surrender vigilance. Rest becomes performative: even leisure is judged by whether it is "earned," "productive," "healthy," or socially presentable. Silence begins to feel suspicious, like a room where something important has been forgotten. You check one more time—not because you want pleasure, but because you want relief. And the relief does not last.

None of this requires melodrama. It requires only the recognition that many of us now live in conditions where the nervous system receives continual signals of incomplete safety. A century ago, people worked brutally hard, but the boundaries between labor and rest were more visible for many. Today, for large numbers of people, work is not merely a place; it is a cloud that follows them. Social pressure is not merely interpersonal; it is algorithmic. Competition is not merely local; it is ambient. Evaluation is not occasional; it is embedded in platforms, institutions, and even the self.

The human animal can adapt to extraordinary hardship. History proves that. But adaptation is not infinite, and it is not free. When the stress response becomes a permanent climate, it stops being a tool and becomes a tax. It consumes energy. It shortens tempers. It dulls curiosity. It turns the mind inward, toward monitoring rather than living. It becomes harder to take pleasure in what is good, because the organism remains preoccupied with what might go wrong.

This is why the language of "coping" often feels subtly insulting. Coping implies that the problem is your inadequate response to life's demands. Yet many people are not failing to cope; they are responding rationally to a system that never truly lets them finish. The issue is not moral weakness. The issue is structural design. We have built lives that ask the nervous system to maintain readiness without resolution, attention without rest, alertness without the dignity of an ending.

The first step toward understanding the human load is not to condemn modernity or idealize the past. It is simply to see the mechanism clearly. A nervous system built for intermittence is now living inside permanence. We are carrying an ancient physiology through a world that increasingly behaves like an endless exam—one in which the questions keep changing, the grading is invisible, and the test never officially concludes.

If life feels heavier than it should, it may be because a part of you is still waiting for the moment when the day is over in the old biological sense: threat passed, tribe safe, fire lit, body downshifting into true recovery. Modern life rarely gives that moment without deliberate boundaries. And even then, it often tries to take it back.

In the chapters ahead, we will widen the lens. We will move from the nervous system to the modern environment: technology as an ecosystem, time as compression, status as perpetual comparison, and meaning as an unexpected form of labor. But we begin here, with the oldest machinery we carry. Not because it explains everything, but because it explains something crucial: why pressure now feels less like a storm and more like weather—and why so many people, even in comfort, feel as if they have not truly exhaled in years.

CHAPTER 2

Small Worlds, Slow Change

A human life is not only a biological life. It is also a social life—lived inside a web of expectations, judgments, loyalties, and shared routines. We tend to think of this web as background. But for most of human history, it was not background at all; it was the structure that held the mind in place. It did not always hold it gently. The past could be brutal, narrow, and unforgiving. Yet it offered something modern life increasingly withholds: a world that was psychologically legible. To live in a small world is to live in a world you can actually *know*.

For most people, most of the time, history was not a drama of constant novelty. It was repetition with variation. The same faces. The same landscape. The same tasks returning with the seasons. The same rituals returning with the calendar. The same moral rules—sometimes wise, sometimes cruel—spoken as if they were as fixed as the stars. Life could be precarious, but it was often predictable in its structure. And predictability, for a nervous system designed for intermittence, is not a luxury. It is a form of rest. The modern mind often underestimates how much equilibrium comes from not having to decide everything.

In a bounded world, identity is not a project; it is largely a given. You do not spend your life inventing yourself from scratch. You are someone's child, someone's sibling, someone's neighbor, someone's apprentice, someone's spouse. Your role is not chosen in the modern sense; it is assigned, inherited, expected. Again: this could be oppressive. It often was. But psychologically, it provided scaffolding. It narrowed the range of possible selves you were required to audition. It reduced the amount of explanation demanded from you.

Modernity praises choice as liberation, and in many ways it is. But choice has a hidden cost that becomes clearer the more the menu expands: **decision load**. Every choice requires attention, comparison, and justification—if not to others, then to oneself. A world that constantly invites you to choose also constantly invites you to doubt. Was that the best decision? The best use of time? The best partner? The best city? The best career? The best diet? The best philosophy? The best self?

When the range of options becomes vast, the mind does not experience this as abundance. It experiences it as a permanent, low-grade problem that never resolves. The modern person is not merely free. The modern person is *responsible*—and not only for actions, but for outcomes, for identity, and even for happiness. This is one of the quiet ways the human load grows. Responsibility expands faster than the nervous system's capacity to carry it.Small worlds also offered another form of relief: limited informational bandwidth.

Most humans historically did not wake up to the awareness of a thousand distant events, scandals, crises, and tragedies. Their emotional attention was largely confined to what happened within walking distance. This was not moral superiority; it was cognitive limitation—and cognitive limitation, in the right dose, is a form of protection. The human mind is capable of empathy, but it is not designed to metabolize global suffering as a daily intake. When the world expands faster than our capacity for emotional processing, compassion begins to fray, and anxiety begins to masquerade as awareness.

Today, the modern person is expected to have opinions about everything, to feel responsible for everything, and to be judged for not caring about everything. This is a new kind of moral pressure: the burden of omniscience without the power of omnipotence. You can know more than any generation before you, and still be helpless in the face of what you know. That helplessness does not remain in the intellect; it migrates into the body. It becomes tension.In a bounded world, time itself had a different texture.

There were natural rhythms that were not negotiated. Day and night mattered. Seasons mattered. Hunger, fatigue, weather, and harvest imposed a tempo. Religious calendars, local customs, and communal rituals punctuated life with shared pauses. One might criticize the superstition and social control embedded in many of these practices. One might rightly reject their exclusions and cruelties. Yet psychologically, these rhythms provided something modernity increasingly erodes: a communal agreement about when life speeds up and when it slows down.

Modern life, by contrast, tends toward frictionless continuity. If you can work anytime, you can work *all the time*. If you can be reached anytime, you can be reached *all the time*. If entertainment is always available, it can be consumed as endlessly as anxiety itself. The old boundaries—between labor and rest, public and private, action and recovery—have thinned. They have not disappeared entirely, but they are now often personal choices rather than shared structures. And personal choices, as we have already seen, are heavy. A world of continuous choice becomes a world of continuous self-performance.

In small worlds, reputation mattered intensely, but it was sustained within a relatively stable community. Today, many people live inside environments of constant evaluation that are both more diffuse and more relentless. You are measured by metrics, reviewed by strangers, judged by online crowds, compared against invisible standards. Even when you are not actively posting or performing, you live with the ambient awareness that performance is possible at any moment. The self becomes a public-facing object, even in private. This produces a subtle form of identity labor: you do not merely live; you monitor how your life would appear if observed.

This is not because people have become vain or shallow. It is because modernity has turned visibility into a currency and legitimacy into a performance. In a small world, legitimacy could be inherited. In the modern world, legitimacy must often be earned repeatedly, displayed publicly, and defended endlessly. And once again the nervous system notices: it reads constant evaluation as constant threat, even when the "threat" is no more than social disapproval or professional uncertainty.

None of this means we should long to return to the past. The bounded worlds of history were frequently violent. They could be trapped in prejudice and hierarchy. They often denied people—especially women, minorities, and the poor—any real autonomy at all. But if we are honest, modernity did not merely remove shackles. It also removed many of the invisible supports that held the mind steady. It replaced shared structure with private management. It replaced communal rhythms with personal scheduling. It replaced inherited identity with self-construction. It replaced limited information with infinite inputs. And it declared that this is what freedom looks like. Freedom is real. So is its cost.

The central point is not nostalgia. It is psychological architecture. Human beings were shaped inside worlds that were small enough to be comprehended and slow enough to be absorbed. That slowness did not make life easy; it made life legible. It allowed the mind to form stable expectations about what mattered and what did not. Modernity, by contrast, multiplies what matters, accelerates change, and demands that each individual continually update their identity, their beliefs, their plans, and their emotional posture toward the world.

This is why modern freedom can feel oddly exhausting. It is not because choice is inherently bad. It is because an unbounded life imposes a kind of permanent cognitive labor: the labor of selecting, comparing, optimizing, and justifying. A person can be liberated from old constraints and still feel overburdened by the new. The mind, once supported by shared structures, now becomes its own manager, its own editor, its own public relations officer. We have not only expanded the world. We have expanded the self's workload.

By the end of this chapter, the reader should see the quiet trade modern life makes. It gives us wider possibilities, broader horizons, and unprecedented mobility. But it also asks us to carry what small worlds carried for us: rhythm, role, meaning, and boundary. In a world of slow change, life was often confined. In a world of rapid change, life becomes open—but openness, without structure, is not always experienced as freedom. It is often experienced as weight.

In the next chapter, we will examine a deeper layer of this weight: the gift and cost of intelligence itself. Because the more the mind can imagine, the more it can worry; the more it can compare, the more it can suffer; and the more it can anticipate, the more it can live inside futures that never arrive. The human load is not only a product of modern systems. It is also a product of what we are: a reflective species living inside an unbounded world.

CHAPTER 3

The Gift and Cost of Intelligence

If the human load were merely a matter of external pressure—deadlines, bills, noise, crowds, technology—then relief would be simple in principle: reduce the pressure and the mind would lighten. Yet anyone who has tried to rest and found their thoughts accelerating in the quiet knows the truth is more complicated. The weight is not only outside us. It is also carried by the very trait that made our species successful: the ability to think beyond the present moment.

Intelligence is not just problem-solving. It is time travel. The most distinctive feature of the human mind is not that it can calculate, but that it can *simulate*. It can project itself into futures that have not happened, revisit past scenes with a fidelity that can wound, and inhabit imagined perspectives—of rivals, lovers, strangers, ancestors, audiences that do not exist. This ability is a gift of extraordinary power. It allows planning, invention, cooperation at scale, and the transmission of knowledge across generations. It is also, quietly, the source of a uniquely human burden: we can suffer not only from what is, but from what might be, what could have been, and what might still be lost.

A deer flees danger and returns, if it survives, to grazing. It does not lie awake rehearsing alternate outcomes. A wolf does not review its mistakes in the manner of a scholar footnoting regret. Human beings do. We are able to turn memory into courtroom testimony, possibility into prophecy, and social perception into a kind of internal surveillance. We carry not only our lives but our interpretations of our lives. We do not merely experience events; we build narratives around them, and then we live inside the narratives.

This is the first way intelligence becomes load-bearing: it expands the range of worlds we can inhabit mentally.In a small world of slow change, this capacity could be stabilizing. Imagination offered myths, songs, rituals, and explanations; foresight offered preparation and prudence. But in the modern world—large, fast, and saturated with information—the same capacity becomes a channel through which pressure floods the mind. The more the mind can model, the more it can worry. The more it can anticipate, the more it can feel endangered by abstract threats. The more it can compare, the more it can feel insufficient.

Modernity does not merely add stimuli. It recruits intelligence as a constant workforce.Consider how many modern systems rely on human anticipation. A person is expected to plan retirement, optimize health, manage career trajectories, maintain social networks, cultivate a brand of competence, remain informed about the world, and navigate bureaucracies that shift without explanation. None of this is intrinsically unreasonable in isolation. The burden arises from accumulation. Modern life increasingly assumes not merely that you can think, but that you can think continuously—strategically, responsibly, and correctly—while the ground shifts under your feet.

This is why the language of "keeping up" feels so apt. The modern mind is expected to be an updating system.And when the mind cannot keep up, it does not simply fail. It becomes anxious. Anxiety is often described as fear without an object. But in many cases it is fear with too many objects—an overload of possible futures, each demanding attention, each whispering that if you were wiser, faster, more disciplined, more informed, you could prevent what you fear.

This is the second way intelligence becomes load-bearing: modern systems exploit it.Not necessarily in a sinister, conspiratorial sense. Exploit here means *use, draw upon, depend on.* Complex societies require planning minds. Markets require calculating minds. Platforms require attentive minds. Institutions require compliant minds that can interpret rules, navigate ambiguity, and absorb blame when the rules contradict themselves. A world that runs on complexity tacitly assumes a population that can continuously process complexity—and then treats the failure to do so as an individual shortcoming.

Even leisure now demands intelligence. To rest used to mean, for many, simply to stop. Today rest often arrives as a project: optimize sleep, optimize diet, optimize exercise, optimize mindfulness, optimize productivity, optimize relationships. The modern person becomes both the patient and the physician, the worker and the manager, the product and the quality-control inspector. When the self is treated as an improvement project, the mind never fully steps off the factory floor. This is where the cost of intelligence becomes most visible: not in thought itself, but in **rumination**—thought that circles without landing.

Planning is healthy. Rumination is planning that has lost its destination. It is anticipation that cannot find a decisive action. It is the mind running simulations not to prepare, but to soothe itself—and failing to be soothed. Modernity supplies endless triggers for this kind of loop: ambiguous social feedback, unclear career prospects, volatile news cycles, financial uncertainty, shifting cultural norms. The reflective mind tries to resolve ambiguity by thinking harder. But ambiguity is not always soluble. Many modern pressures do not have solutions; they have management strategies. When intelligence tries to turn management into resolution, it becomes stuck.

The result is a peculiar modern pathology: the mind becomes a place of work rather than a place of experience. This is not because intelligence is "bad." Intelligence is the reason we have art, science, civilization, and moral reflection. But intelligence is not costless. It magnifies whatever conditions it lives within. In a stable world, reflection can deepen meaning. In an unstable world, reflection can become a burden. Intelligence can create freedom—but it can also create a prison made of possibilities.

There is a further irony. Modern life promises mastery through information. Yet the more information we possess, the less certainty we often feel. This is the paradox of the age: more data, more choices, more expert commentary, more predictions—yet a growing sense of fragility. The reflective mind absorbs not only facts but second-order knowledge: knowledge about how uncertain knowledge is. It learns that experts disagree, that systems are complex, that unintended consequences are common, that models fail. This is intellectually honest, but psychologically heavy. A person can be informed and still feel unmoored, because information is not the same as orientation.

And when orientation collapses, intelligence works overtime to compensate.This is where self-awareness becomes another form of load. Self-awareness is often praised as maturity, and it can be. But in the modern environment it is easily turned into **self-surveillance**. You do not merely act; you watch yourself acting. You do not merely speak; you monitor how your speech might be received. You do not merely live; you curate the appearance of your life, even if no one is watching at that moment. The self becomes both actor and audience, and the audience is rarely kind.

In earlier ages, shame was often imposed externally by small communities. Today shame can be internalized and automated. The reflective mind becomes capable of generating its own tribunal: a running commentary of how one is doing, how one is failing, how one is perceived, how one should be improved. The ability to evaluate oneself—so valuable for growth—becomes, when overactivated, a source of continuous pressure.

Modernity has learned to monetize this. Platforms thrive on comparison, aspiration, and the sense that you are one upgrade away from adequacy. Institutions thrive on metrics that keep you striving for the next benchmark. Even the language of self-development can become a trap: you are never simply a person; you are a project. None of this would work on a species that could not imagine alternate selves and alternate futures. It works precisely because humans can. It works because intelligence, once recruited, is difficult to switch off.

This is why modern life weighs heaviest on the reflective mind. Some people suffer from poverty and instability; their load is obvious and severe. Others suffer in comfort, and their suffering is harder to explain, even to themselves. They have food, shelter, safety—and yet they feel strained. Often what they are carrying is not deprivation but cognition. They are carrying the invisible labor of constant evaluation, constant planning, constant comparison, constant updating, constant self-management. Their mind is busy not because life is dramatic, but because life is unbounded.

The answer is not to despise intelligence or pretend that ignorance is a cure. The goal is not to romanticize simplicity or mock reflection. The goal is to see the trade honestly: intelligence gives us worlds, and it asks us to carry them. It gives us foresight, and it burdens us with futures. It gives us moral imagination, and it burdens us with responsibility. It gives us freedom of choice, and it burdens us with the need to justify our choices—not only to others, but to ourselves.

In the chapters that follow, we will examine how modern systems amplify this cost. Technology intensifies comparison and accelerates time. Status pressure turns identity into performance. Infinite information erodes certainty while demanding constant opinion. Meaning, once inherited, becomes a private project. But beneath all these pressures lies a deeper fact: the human mind is powerful enough to build civilization—and sensitive enough to be strained by it.

A reflective species can create astonishing complexity. It can also be exhausted by its own creation.

Part II — The Six Pressures

CHAPTER 4

Chronic Stress: Life Without Resolution

The modern person does not live in a constant emergency. Yet many modern people live as if something is always pending, suspended in a state that never quite resolves. This sense of incompletion is not dramatic or catastrophic, but it is persistent enough to shape how the body and mind experience ordinary days.

That word—*pending*—captures a great deal of what has changed. Not because our lives are uniquely tragic, but because they are uniquely unfinished. We move through days filled with tasks that do not conclude but merely convert into more tasks, and this conversion happens so seamlessly that it begins to feel natural.

We respond, update, comply, schedule, optimize, pay, confirm, submit, check, and follow up. We do this so frequently that we begin to mistake this maintenance for life itself. And when we finally sit down to rest, we discover that rest does not behave the way it once did, because the organism has not received a clear signal that the work is done.

The body may be quiet, but the mind remains braced. The organism does not feel endangered, yet it refuses to stand down, as though it were waiting for an instruction that never arrives. This is where chronic stress becomes something more precise than a mood or a feeling. It becomes an architecture.

Stress, in its original biological sense, is not supposed to be a lifestyle. It is a mechanism for survival—short activation followed by recovery. The body surges, focuses, mobilizes, and then returns, and this return is not optional but essential.

The cycle is as important as the surge. Without the return, the system does not merely stay "on"; it begins to degrade under its own operating costs. The problem modern life creates is not that it triggers stress, but that it triggers stress while systematically interrupting recovery.

The harm is not drama; the harm is duration. A dramatic event can be endured if it resolves, while a persistent low-grade pressure becomes corrosive precisely because it does not. Many modern stressors are not acute dangers but chronic uncertainties that linger rather than conclude.

They rarely provide the closure the nervous system is waiting for. Even success often fails to supply relief, because success becomes a new baseline and the baseline becomes a new demand. What the body experiences is not triumph, but escalation.

This is why chronic stress should be understood less as an emotion and more as a pattern. It is the repeated failure of loops to close, the accumulation of signals that say "not finished yet." Over time, the organism learns to remain vigilant by default.

Consider the simplest emblem of modern life: the inbox. An email can be answered, but the inbox itself cannot be finished; at best, it can be managed. This distinction matters psychologically, because the mind treats open loops as unfinished business, and unfinished business reliably activates vigilance.

The inbox is not merely annoying; it is instructive. It teaches the nervous system that effort does not lead to completion, only to temporary reprieve. And the inbox is only the visible tip of a much larger phenomenon.

Modern life is filled with systems that behave like bottomless containers. Feeds never end, lists regenerate, responsibilities renew, standards escalate, and information multiplies. The stress response evolved for environments in which action produced resolution, not for systems in which action sustains the system itself.

You act and the system remains. You pay and the bills return. You comply and the rules update. You improve and the benchmark moves. The modern person is not merely working; the modern person is maintaining.

This maintenance is not always oppressive, and much of it is necessary. But it has a cumulative effect that is easy to miss because each individual demand appears small. A single message is small, a single payment is small, a single reminder is small, yet a life made of small demands is still a life made of demands.

Because many of these demands are social or bureaucratic rather than physical, they do not burn themselves out through exertion. Instead, they linger in the mind as unresolved signals: something still needs attention, something could still go wrong, something is still being assessed. The nervous system responds accordingly.

This is why rest fails in a way that feels almost insulting. You lie down, but your mind does not follow you, because it has not received confirmation that vigilance is no longer required. The body interprets rest as premature.

Chronic stress often announces itself through this quiet betrayal. The person is not in crisis; they are in a state of perpetual readiness. The body is not sprinting; it is idling too high, consuming energy simply by staying prepared.

The mind is not panicking; it is scanning. In such a state, even leisure can feel tense, because leisure is not experienced as safety but as vulnerability. Unstructured time becomes a space in which you might be discovered to be behind, unprepared, or negligent.

This is one reason the modern Sunday evening has acquired its own emotional signature. It is not fear and not sadness, but a tightening—a sense that obligations are about to reassert themselves. The organism braces not for a predator but for a calendar.

A second major engine of chronic stress is financial uncertainty, which in modern life often persists even among those who are not poor. The uncertainty may involve employment, housing, healthcare, inflation, family obligations, or the fear that one mistake could cascade into something irreversible. Even when resources are sufficient, psychological safety may not be.

The mind does not ask, "Am I safe today?" It asks, "Will I remain safe next year?" and "Will my position hold?" Because these questions cannot be conclusively answered, the stress system remains engaged.

A third engine is ambient evaluation. Earlier societies evaluated people harshly and intimately, but modern evaluation has a different character: it is continuous, quantified, and detached from human relationship. Ratings, reviews, metrics, surveillance, analytics, and digital reputations create an atmosphere in which evaluation is always possible.

To be evaluated occasionally is a burden. To live inside a climate where evaluation never fully switches off is something else entirely. The nervous system treats this as a standing social threat.

This is why chronic stress can feel disproportionate to events. A person may say, truthfully, that nothing terrible has happened, yet the body behaves as if something might. Modern systems distribute risk across countless small contingencies, none catastrophic alone, but together sufficient to prevent the feeling of safety from ever settling.

Relief becomes temporary, while vigilance becomes default. At this point it is tempting to medicalize the experience, to treat it as an individual disorder. But a more honest interpretation is that much of chronic stress is a reasonable response to an environment designed to keep people responsive, engaged, and self-monitoring.

The system wants attention, compliance, participation, aspiration, and availability. None of this requires malice; it only requires incentives. And because it requires no villain, it is harder to resist.

This is why chronic stress belongs under the concept of *load* rather than pathology. Load does not mean something is broken; it means something is being carried continuously. Chronic stress is what happens when carrying becomes permanent and recovery becomes optional.

By the end of this chapter, the reader should feel a shift in interpretation. If life feels heavy, it may not be because of personal weakness or failure of resilience. It may be because modern life offers effort without completion, responsiveness without closure, and activity without downshift.

The body is not protesting life; it is reacting to a life that rarely ends the way the body expects a day to end. The organism still waits for the old signal: essential tasks done, danger passed, tomorrow not already due.

In the next chapter, we will examine a major amplifier of this condition: technology. Not because technology is malicious, but because it creates environments in which loops are never meant to close, feeds are never meant to end, and incompletion quietly becomes normal.

CHAPTER 5

Technological Saturation: Tools Become Environments

For most of human history, tools were things you picked up and put down. A knife cut, a hammer struck, a loom wove, and when the task was finished the tool receded from attention. The mind returned to its broader field of experience, no longer shaped by the instrument it had just used.

Modern technology behaves differently. It does not wait to be picked up, and it does not easily recede. It surrounds, persists, and increasingly defines the background conditions of everyday life.

This shift—from tool to environment—is one of the most important yet least examined sources of the modern human load. Technology is no longer something we use intermittently; it is something we live inside. It shapes not only what we do, but how we think, how we allocate attention, and how we experience time and selfhood.

The distinction matters because environments train organisms whether they intend to or not. A forest trains a body to notice movement and sound, while a city trains it to filter noise and navigate density. A digital environment trains the mind to remain alert, interruptible, and responsive, even when nothing urgent is happening.

It does this not through force, but through design. Modern technologies are optimized to be frictionless, immediate, and engaging, qualities that feel helpful and efficient on the surface. Yet these same qualities also determine how attention is captured, held, and fragmented.

Attention, however, is not an infinite resource. It is a biological capacity with limits, rhythms, and recovery needs, even if those limits are rarely acknowledged. When attention is treated as endlessly renewable, the organism quietly absorbs the cost.

One of the defining features of technological saturation is fragmentation. Notifications, alerts, updates, messages, reminders, and prompts divide attention into smaller and smaller units across the day. Each interruption may be minor and even useful, but the cumulative effect is substantial.

Fragmented attention produces a peculiar fatigue. It is not the exhaustion of effort, but the weariness of constant reorientation. The mind is repeatedly pulled away from what it was doing and asked to reset, reassess, and reengage, often without completing any of those processes fully.

This resetting has a cost that is easy to underestimate. When attention is fractured, tasks take longer, errors increase, and irritation rises, even when overall workload appears reasonable. The organism experiences this not as a clear problem but as a background drain, a sense of being worn down without knowing why.

People often describe this state as being tired for no reason or feeling inexplicably on edge. What they are experiencing is the metabolic and cognitive cost of sustained interruption. In such conditions, the mind rarely settles into depth and rarely descends fully into rest.

Depth requires continuity, and continuity requires protection. Saturation undermines both by normalizing interruption and treating responsiveness as a virtue. Over time, the mind adapts by remaining shallow and vigilant rather than deep and absorbed.

Technological environments also collapse boundaries that once provided psychological relief. Work, for many people, was once a place you went and a time you entered. Now it is a cloud that follows, extending into evenings, weekends, and spaces that once belonged to recovery.

Messages arrive outside formal hours, and expectations leak into moments previously understood as personal or private. Even when no one is actively demanding attention, the possibility remains. The nervous system responds to possibility as if it were pressure, because possibility still requires readiness.

This is how convenience quietly becomes obligation. The ability to respond quickly turns into the expectation to respond quickly, and the expectation hardens into a standard. Once the standard becomes invisible, it is enforced not by supervisors or systems, but by the individual's own sense of risk and responsibility.

People check not because they are commanded to, but because not checking feels negligent. The line between choice and compulsion blurs through repetition rather than coercion. What remains is a state of constant availability.

Availability is a subtle burden because it rarely announces itself as work. You are not actively doing anything, yet you are not fully off duty either. The mind remains partially open, listening for the signal that it is needed, and that posture carries a metabolic cost.

This low-grade readiness mirrors chronic stress even when actual demands are light. The organism consumes energy simply by staying prepared. Over time, this erodes the feeling of safety that rest depends on.

Another feature of technological saturation is the transformation of judgment. Modern tools offer guidance constantly, telling you where to go, what to choose, what is valued, and how you are performing. In many cases this guidance is genuinely helpful and reduces uncertainty.

But when guidance becomes ubiquitous, it can quietly erode confidence in one's own perception and decision-making. Judgment, like attention, is a muscle that strengthens through use and weakens through outsourcing. When choices are always pre-structured, ranked, and optimized, the individual learns to defer rather than decide.

Over time, this produces a subtle dependency. The person may feel informed but less certain, assisted but less assured. The paradox becomes visible: more information, less confidence.

The mind grows crowded with inputs but deprived of the experience of arriving at conclusions through its own internal process. This contributes to the human load by replacing trust in judgment with reliance on systems that can never fully account for context or values.

Technological environments also amplify comparison, not necessarily by intent but by visibility. Lives, achievements, opinions, and identities are placed in constant view, turning comparison into a background activity rather than a deliberate one. Even when people know intellectually that what they see is curated, the emotional system responds as if it were representative.

Comparison, once localized, becomes planetary. This expansion breaks the scale at which human psychology evolved to operate. The mind is drawn into comparisons it cannot resolve, against standards it cannot meet, within systems it cannot exit without social or professional cost.

The result is not sustained motivation but gradual erosion. A persistent sense of inadequacy emerges without a clear source and therefore resists correction. The pressure is ambient rather than acute, and that makes it harder to name and harder to escape.

None of this requires bad actors or malicious intent. The pressure arises from alignment rather than conspiracy. Technologies are optimized for engagement because engagement sustains them, and speed is rewarded because speed increases throughput.

Responsiveness is praised because it signals competence, reliability, and relevance. Each incentive is reasonable in isolation. Together, they create an environment that extracts continuous attention from a finite organism.

This is why technological saturation can exhaust even when it helps. A navigation system can save time and still increase cognitive dependence. A communication platform can connect people and still fragment attention.

A productivity tool can streamline tasks and still multiply expectations. The benefits are real, and so are the costs. The human load increases not because technology fails, but because it succeeds too well at what it is designed to do.

The question, then, is not whether technology is good or bad. That question is too blunt to be useful. The more precise question is whether the environments we have built respect the limits of the human nervous system or quietly assume capacities for attention, availability, and self-regulation that exceed what biology can sustainably provide.

When tools become environments, disengagement becomes effortful. Silence becomes unusual, and unreachability begins to feel irresponsible rather than restorative. The mind learns to treat constant input as normal and absence as risk.

In such a world, rest must be defended rather than assumed. Presence must be practiced rather than given. The human load grows not through catastrophe, but through saturation.

In the next chapter, we will turn to time itself. Because once speed becomes the norm and responsiveness becomes expected, time no longer feels like the medium in which life unfolds. It begins to feel like something that is always running out, even as it is being saved.

CHAPTER 6

Time Compression: Acceleration Without Arrival

One of the strangest features of modern life is that it is filled with time-saving devices, yet saturated with the feeling of time scarcity. We can communicate instantly, travel faster, automate routine tasks, and retrieve information in seconds. Yet many people feel as if they are always running behind, always catching up, and always living one step away from the moment they can finally exhale.

This is not merely a scheduling problem. It is a structural feature of a civilization that converts speed into expectation and expectation into pressure. Time is being saved, but the savings are rarely returned to the person in the form of spaciousness. They are reinvested into throughput.

In earlier eras, many tasks were slow by necessity, and slowness imposed a kind of order. Letters took days or weeks, and the gap between sending and receiving created a buffer that protected attention and emotion. Travel took time, and the journey itself acted as a boundary between places and roles. Work had rhythms that often-forced natural stopping points, even when the labor was harsh.

Modern technology removes many of those buffers, and the removal is often celebrated as progress. The problem is not that this progress is false. The problem is that buffers were doing psychological work that modern systems rarely replace. When friction disappears, the mind is asked to operate at higher speed without the recovery periods that friction quietly provided.

Speed does not merely change how quickly we do things. It changes what we are expected to do, and it changes how quickly we are expected to do it. Once communication becomes instant, the pace of response becomes the new baseline.

A message that once could be answered tomorrow now carries the subtle expectation of being answered soon. “Soon” becomes “today,” and “today” becomes “now,” not through explicit demand but through cultural drift. People begin to feel negligent for moving at a human pace in a system that can move faster.

The compression happens gradually, but its effects accumulate. A faster world produces more micro-obligations: acknowledgments, confirmations, follow-ups, updates, and the quiet requirement to stay informed. Each one is small, and that is precisely why they are dangerous. They slip beneath moral attention, but they still consume time and fragment thought.

Time compression is therefore not simply about having too much to do. It is also about how modernity slices life into smaller units of attention and turns those units into currency. When time is divided into fragments, experience loses depth.

You may do more in a day, but you inhabit less of what you do. The mind is repeatedly shifted from one context to another, and each shift carries a cognitive cost. The day becomes a chain of transitions rather than a field of sustained presence.

This produces a distinctive modern fatigue. It is not only the tiredness of long hours. It is the fatigue of constant switching, constant reorientation, and constant partial attention. The mind becomes busy, yet strangely unfulfilled, because it has been moving quickly without arriving anywhere.

Acceleration without arrival is the feeling of doing a great deal while living very little. It is the sensation of motion without culmination, of activity without the deep satisfaction that comes from immersion. The body may be at rest at the end of the day, but the mind feels as though it never truly landed.

It is tempting to blame individuals for poor time management, and there are certainly personal habits that can make life worse. But the deeper truth is that time compression is a system feature. Modern institutions and technologies are designed to increase throughput, and throughput reshapes the lived experience of time. Once speed is possible, it becomes competitive, and once it becomes competitive, it becomes quietly compulsory.

Even leisure is absorbed into this logic. Leisure once existed, for many people, as a time of unstructured recovery. Today leisure is often treated as a project, monitored and optimized the way work is monitored and optimized. People track sleep, track exercise, track steps, track calories, track reading goals, track the number of countries visited, and track the number of experiences consumed.

Even relaxation is judged by whether it is effective. The result is that rest becomes another domain of performance. The mind does not stop evaluating; it simply evaluates a different category. A person may be off work and still feel pressured, because the deeper pressure is not work itself. The deeper pressure is the sense that time must be used correctly, that every hour carries an opportunity cost, and that a good life is something one must constantly manage.

Time scarcity becomes not only practical but moral. This moralization of time is one of the sharpest ways modernity adds to the human load. When time is moralized, idleness feels like guilt. Slowness feels like failure, and saying no feels risky because it may mean falling behind.

Because the benchmarks of modern life are often vague, comparative, and socially mediated, the mind rarely receives the reassurance that it has done enough. There is always more that could have been done, and modern systems make that "more" visible at all times. The world presents itself as a permanent menu of tasks, improvements, and options, and the mind experiences the menu as pressure.

This visibility deepens the compression. You can see other people being productive, other people traveling, other people improving, other people publishing, other people responding, and other people optimizing. You can see opportunities you did not take, articles you did not read, messages you did not answer, and skills you have not acquired. The world becomes a catalogue of missed options, and the mind registers that catalogue as evidence of inadequacy.

In earlier ages, ignorance was often unavoidable. Today ignorance feels like negligence, because knowledge is always available. Yet availability is not the same as capacity, and a person can access infinite information while possessing only finite attention. The gap between what could be known and what can be known produces a quiet anxiety that attaches itself to time, because time becomes the bottleneck through which everything must pass.

Time compression therefore does not merely make life fast; it makes life evaluative. The day becomes a ledger, hours become units to be accounted for, and the person becomes their own auditor. This is why many people feel that modern life is not only busy but brittle.

There is little slack, little margin, and little unstructured space where errors can be absorbed and the mind can wander without punishment.

Slack is not inefficiency, and it is not moral weakness. Slack is what makes a system resilient. Human beings need slack for thinking, for creativity, for emotional digestion, and for the restoration of attention. Without slack, life becomes a form of continuous triage: you deal with what is urgent, then you deal with what is next, and the long-term questions—meaning, direction, depth—are postponed indefinitely. The mind may be full, but it is not nourished.

This is why the modern person can feel perpetually behind even when accomplishing a great deal. The speed of the system becomes the speed of expectation, and the speed of expectation becomes the internal voice that says you are late, even when you are doing your best. Time is saved, but the savings are claimed by the system, and the individual experiences the result as scarcity rather than freedom.

The point is not to declare speed evil. Speed is often lifesaving, and the ability to communicate and coordinate rapidly is one of civilization's great achievements. The point is to name the trade honestly. Speed changes not only what is possible, but what is demanded. In a world of acceleration, the human mind is asked to operate as if it were frictionless, endlessly updateable, and always ready, and it is none of those things.

In the next chapter, we will examine another form of pressure that intensifies time compression and feeds on it: economic and status anxiety. Once time becomes a moral and competitive resource, the fear of falling behind stops being metaphorical. It becomes a quiet terror that organizes modern lives and turns speed into a form of social survival.

CHAPTER 7

Economic & Status Pressure: The Quiet Terror of Falling Behind

In modern life, money is rarely just money. It is security, autonomy, and insulation from uncertainty, and it is also something more elusive: a proxy for competence, a signal of worth, and a measure of whether one is keeping pace with the world one inhabits. This is why economic pressure can burden people who are poor in obvious ways and people who are comfortable in quieter ones. The load is not simply the fear of not having enough; it is the fear of falling behind in a system where "enough" is never clearly defined.

Status has always mattered, but modern status behaves differently. In small communities, status was often stable, local, and tied to known roles. Today status is fluid, comparative, and continuously updated, and the mechanisms that track it are often impersonal. People are scored, ranked, reviewed, credentialed, followed, measured, and compared, and even when these measurements are not explicit they are felt as a background expectation. The social world becomes a field of evaluation in which the self is not simply living but performing.

Economic and status pressure also intensify one another. Economic insecurity sharpens status anxiety, because status is often a form of protection against future loss. Status anxiety sharpens economic insecurity, because the fear is not merely poverty but descent. Modern life therefore does not merely ask people to survive; it asks them to maintain position, and maintenance in a competitive environment is an endless task.

This is one reason modern work so often expands beyond its practical function. Work is not merely the means by which society produces goods and services. It becomes identity, narrative, and moral standing. Many people do not simply have jobs; they have public evidence that they are legitimate. When work is treated as proof of worth, the threat of instability becomes existential. Losing a position can feel like losing a self, because the culture has trained people to fuse contribution with identity and identity with value.

A system built on competition does not require cruelty to create pressure. It requires only visibility and comparison, because comparison produces a permanent sense of insufficiency. In an environment where there is always someone richer, more accomplished, more admired, or more "optimized," the mind experiences success as temporary and vulnerability as constant. The person is not merely trying to improve; the person is trying to avoid decline, and the fear of decline is one of the strongest engines of chronic vigilance.

The modern economy also amplifies the load by making long-term planning mandatory while making long-term certainty elusive. Earlier lives were often precarious, but the causes of precarity were visible: weather, harvest, illness, war, and local conflict. Modern precarity can be more abstract: inflation, market volatility, automation, institutional shifts, layoffs, policy changes, and the quiet instability of systems that are too complex for any individual to understand. The reflective mind responds to abstraction by trying to model it, but modeling does not produce control. The result is a peculiar form of anxiety: responsibility without agency.

This is one reason financial pressure feels different from physical hardship. Physical hardship is immediate and exhausting, but it can be psychologically direct. Financial pressure is often anticipatory. It recruits the future continuously. It pushes the mind to run simulations: what if the job changes, what if the cost rises, what if the market falls, what if health fails, what if a family member needs help, what if the safety net is thinner than expected. Each "what if" is a thread, and modern life offers thousands of them.

Status pressure is not confined to money, but money is one of its most effective accelerants because it turns comparison into arithmetic. Even among people who claim not to care about status, status remains present because it is embedded in systems that distribute respect, attention, and opportunity. Credentials function as gates. Titles function as signals. Brands function as shorthand for taste and legitimacy. Even moral positions can function as status markers, because social approval is a currency the mind is trained to track. The result is that modern life becomes a sequence of auditions, some explicit and many unspoken.

This audition culture is one of the least discussed sources of fatigue in contemporary societies. When evaluation is constant, the self becomes cautious and strategic. People begin to manage impressions, soften statements, frame identities, and curate affiliations, not because they are dishonest but because the environment punishes missteps and rewards conformity. The person learns to think not only "What do I believe?" but "How will this be received?" That extra layer of self-monitoring is not merely social; it is physiological. It keeps the nervous system slightly activated because social risk is still risk.

The pressure also spreads into areas that appear unrelated to economics. Bodies become status objects. Experiences become status objects. Travel becomes status. Fitness becomes status. Even simplicity becomes status when it is performed as superiority. Modernity does not merely expand the field of competition; it makes competition portable. The individual carries it everywhere, because comparison is no longer limited to a workplace or a neighborhood. It is embedded in feeds, metrics, and ambient cultural messaging that subtly instructs the person to keep upgrading, keep improving, and keep displaying.

It is important to acknowledge that economic pressure is not evenly distributed. For many people, it is not a matter of subtle anxiety but of relentless material constraint, and the human load in such cases is heavy in the most literal sense. Yet one reason this chapter matters is that status pressure does not disappear with comfort. In some ways, comfort can intensify it, because the fear shifts from survival to decline, and decline is experienced as humiliation. The mind becomes protective of what it has built, and protective vigilance is exhausting.

Modern economic systems also create a particular kind of insecurity by attaching basic stability to performance. When healthcare, housing, education, and retirement are increasingly expensive and competitive, people experience life as a high-stakes balancing act. The stakes do not need to be catastrophic to be felt as constant. A person can be doing well and still feel one mistake away from consequences, and that feeling keeps the body in partial readiness.

This is why the economic and status pressures of modernity are inseparable from the broader theme of load. They convert life into a treadmill not merely because people are greedy, but because systems are structured to turn stability into a prize rather than a floor. When stability must be earned repeatedly, the organism never fully relaxes. It learns that rest is risky because rest is time that could have been used to secure position.

The deeper tragedy is that this pressure is often sold as motivation. The culture suggests that constant striving is the engine of progress and the mark of virtue. Yet striving becomes corrosive when it is no longer directed toward meaningful ends but toward the avoidance of falling behind. At that point, ambition is no longer aspiration; it is defense. The person may appear successful from the outside while feeling perpetually behind from the inside, because the benchmark keeps moving and the comparison never ends.

In the next chapter, we will examine the most powerful amplifier of this dynamic: social comparison at planetary scale. Economic and status pressure are heavy enough within a local community. When comparison expands to a global feed of curated lives and algorithmic extremes, the mind loses the ability to locate "enough." The result is not merely dissatisfaction, but a persistent sense that adequacy itself has become unreachable.

CHAPTER 8

Social Comparison at Planetary Scale

Human beings have always compared themselves to others. Comparison is not a modern invention and not a moral defect. It is a social instinct with deep evolutionary roots, helping individuals locate their status, refine behavior, and maintain belonging within a group. In a small community, comparison had limits. You compared yourself to a finite set of known people, living under roughly similar conditions, within a shared horizon of what life could reasonably be.

Modernity has removed those limits. Comparison has been scaled beyond the human frame. The change is not only that we now see more people. The change is that we now see more lives, more curated narratives, more achievements, more beauty, more wealth, more outrage, and more ideological certainty than a human mind was ever meant to absorb as daily input. The village has been replaced by a planetary display window, and the mind responds to what it sees even when it knows it should not.

This is one of the most corrosive sources of modern load because it attacks the feeling of adequacy at its roots. A person does not need to be poor to feel insufficient. A person does not need to be unsuccessful to feel behind. All that is required is exposure to a constant stream of people who seem, in one way or another, to be doing better, living better, looking better, traveling more, achieving more, or holding more certainty about their identity and purpose.

The crucial word here is "seem." Much of what is visible is curated, edited, filtered, and staged, whether consciously or by the incentives of the platforms themselves. Yet the emotional system does not treat curated images as hypotheticals. It treats them as social data. The rational mind may say, "This is a highlight reel," but the deeper mind still feels the comparison. It still registers that others appear happier, more fulfilled, more admired, and more complete.

This mismatch between knowledge and feeling is part of what makes comparison so exhausting. People are asked to be both human and immune to being human. They are expected to consume endless social information without allowing it to shape self-evaluation. The expectation is unrealistic. In the end, the mind either absorbs the pressure or numbs itself, and both responses carry cost.

Planetary comparison also distorts norms. In a small world, extremes were rare and socially bounded. In a digital world, extremes are rewarded because they are more visible, more shareable, and more emotionally activating. The result is that the mind begins to treat extremes as typical, even when it knows intellectually that they are not. Wealth at the top becomes the reference point for "success." Beauty at the most engineered end becomes the reference point for "normal." Achievement at the most relentless end becomes the reference point for "productivity."

This distortion does not merely create envy. It creates instability in the sense of what counts as enough. The mind was not designed to live in a world where the reference group is infinite. In a village, you could reach a plateau of social comparison because the best hunter, the most admired elder, the most talented storyteller, and the most prosperous family were known and finite. Today the reference group never ends. There is always someone more extreme, and therefore the ladder never reaches a top. Even if you climb, you still feel as if you are at the bottom, because the ladder extends endlessly upward.

This is one reason modern life can produce a constant sense of striving without satisfaction. Satisfaction depends on closure, and closure requires a boundary. Planetary comparison removes the boundary. It turns improvement into an infinite game, and infinite games are psychologically costly when the stakes feel personal.

Visibility also changes the nature of social life. In a bounded community, one's social existence was largely interpersonal. You were known by people who could see you in context. In modern environments, social existence increasingly resembles performance before an audience. The audience may be abstract, intermittent, or invisible, but the possibility of being observed shapes behavior. People begin to curate their lives, not merely for vanity, but for safety and belonging. Identity becomes something to present, refine, and defend.

This introduces a new layer of labor: identity management. A person is not only living; they are considering how their life looks. They are not only forming beliefs; they are calibrating which beliefs are acceptable within the social environments they inhabit. They are not only speaking; they are monitoring what their speech will signal. The result is a continuous low-grade pressure that resembles stage fright, except the stage has no exit.

Planetary comparison also changes the moral atmosphere. When views are public, morality becomes performative. People begin to signal virtue to maintain belonging, and they begin to treat disagreement as contamination. This does not mean that moral concern is fake. It means that moral concern can become entangled with status, because social approval is still a currency the mind is trained to track. The person's ethical life is therefore pressured from two sides: the desire to be good and the desire to be seen as good.

The cost of this entanglement is constant vigilance. The mind watches not only what it does, but what it appears to do. It anticipates judgment. It rehearses explanations. It scans for social danger. The person becomes both actor and audience, and the audience is often hostile, because modern audiences are not communities. They are crowds. Crowds do not forgive the way communities sometimes can.

It is important to say, again, that comparison is not inherently pathological. Comparison can motivate learning, improve social coordination, and help individuals locate themselves. The problem is scale. The problem is that comparison has been enlarged beyond human proportions and then fed to the mind as continuous stimulus. A system that constantly displays superior examples will produce constant feelings of inferiority, even among people who are objectively doing well.

This is why the modern person often cannot locate adequacy. Adequacy is not a number or a title; it is a feeling of being within the acceptable range of one's social world. When the social world becomes planetary and algorithmically curated toward extremes, the acceptable range becomes unreachable. The mind loses its sense of where it stands, because the floor and ceiling are constantly moving.

The result is not simply envy, but erosion. It erodes gratitude, because gratitude requires presence and sufficiency. It erodes joy, because joy becomes fragile when it is immediately compared. It erodes identity, because identity becomes an ongoing project of adjustment rather than a stable experience of being. It erodes social trust, because people begin to interpret others not as peers but as competitors or judges.

This helps explain why so many people feel socially saturated and yet socially lonely. They are surrounded by images of others, yet deprived of the stabilizing warmth of real belonging. They are exposed to endless social information, yet still feel unseen. The mind is flooded with representation but starved of relationship, and the cost of that mismatch is heavy.

In the next chapter, we will move from comparison to meaning. Because once comparison becomes infinite and identity becomes performance, the question of purpose changes character. Meaning stops being something quietly inherited through shared frameworks, and it becomes something the individual is expected to manufacture alone. When meaning becomes work, modern life acquires a new pressure that cannot be solved by productivity, because it is not a task. It is an existential demand.

CHAPTER 9

Meaning as Work: Freedom Without Shared Metaphysics

Modern life does not only demand that people manage schedules, careers, finances, and attention. It demands something deeper and more difficult to articulate: it demands that people assemble a reason for living, and do so as an individual project. This demand is often framed as liberation. Few of us would willingly return to worlds where meaning was enforced by rigid hierarchy, coercive custom, or inherited constraint. Yet it is possible to reject those worlds and still recognize a cost in what replaced them. When shared frameworks weaken, the burden of meaning does not disappear. It migrates inward. Meaning becomes work.

In many traditional societies, meaning was not primarily something one invented. It was something one received, through religion, community, role, and rhythm. The frameworks were often incomplete and frequently unjust, but they provided orientation. They told people, in broad strokes, what a good life was, what duties mattered, what suffering meant, and how a person should locate themselves within the universe. Individuals could struggle within these frameworks, and many did, but the framework itself offered a kind of psychological scaffolding. It reduced the need to justify existence from scratch.

Modernity expands freedom by loosening inherited scripts. It gives people unprecedented latitude to choose how they live, what they believe, where they go, and who they become. That freedom is real and often precious. Yet freedom also introduces a new form of responsibility: the responsibility to construct a coherent self and a coherent life without the stabilizing authority of a shared metaphysical map.

The modern person is often told to "find your purpose." This sounds inspiring, but it also functions as a command. It suggests that meaning is something you must discover through effort, and if you have not discovered it, the deficiency is yours. In earlier worlds, a person could be miserable but still feel that their life belonged to a larger structure. In modern worlds, a person can be comfortable and still feel unmoored, because comfort is not the same as meaning and choice is not the same as orientation.

This is one reason modern success can feel strangely thin. People can achieve what they once believed they wanted and still experience a hollowing out, not because they are ungrateful but because achievement does not automatically answer existential questions. A life can be efficient, impressive, and socially validated and still feel as if it lacks a center. When the center is missing, the mind tries to manufacture it. That manufacturing is labor.

It is labor because it never fully ends. A person can build a career, but purpose still demands justification. A person can build a family, but meaning still demands interpretation. A person can adopt a philosophy, but doubt still returns, because modernity teaches the mind that alternatives are always available. The sheer availability of alternatives makes the chosen path feel contingent, and contingency makes meaning feel fragile.

This fragility is intensified by the modern expectation that identity should be self-designed. In earlier societies, identity was often imposed, sometimes cruelly. Modernity rightly resists that imposition. Yet it replaces it with a new pressure: you must become someone by deliberate construction, and you must continue refining that construction throughout life. Identity becomes a project rather than a condition, and projects are evaluated.

The evaluation is partly social, but it is also internal. People learn to ask not only "Who am I?" but "Is my identity coherent, admirable, and defensible?" They learn to curate their values the way they curate their choices, because values are now signals as well as convictions. In a world of public visibility, meaning becomes something that must not only be lived but displayed. This is why meaning increasingly resembles performance.

The pressure can also become therapeutic. Modern culture often encourages people to treat the self as a continuous improvement project, subject to constant analysis and correction. Self-knowledge can be valuable, and psychological language can illuminate hidden patterns. Yet when self-analysis becomes endless, it does not liberate. It becomes another form of monitoring. The person's inner life is treated as a system to optimize rather than a reality to inhabit.

This is an especially subtle form of load because it masquerades as progress. A person may believe they are becoming wiser while actually becoming more anxious, simply because the mind has been trained to treat every discomfort as a problem requiring diagnosis. Meaning becomes a form of maintenance, and maintenance, as we have seen, is rarely complete.

The paradox is that the modern world offers more opportunities than ever before, yet the abundance of opportunity can weaken commitment. A commitment is a closing of possibilities. It is a decision to live within chosen limits. Modern culture often hesitates to celebrate limits, because limits sound like constraint and constraint sounds like oppression. Yet without chosen limits, life becomes a perpetually open file. And an open file generates anxiety.

This is why meaning as work is inseparable from the earlier chapters on time compression and comparison. When time feels scarce, people feel pressured to use it "correctly." When comparison is infinite, people feel pressured to choose identities and paths that will be socially legible. When technology saturates attention, people struggle to sustain the depth required for meaning to form. The modern person is therefore asked to build purpose in an environment that continually disrupts purpose-making.

Meaning does not arise from constant stimulation. It arises from continuity, reflection, and belonging. A world of perpetual input starves those conditions while pretending to enhance them.

It is also important to note that meaning has become politicized and moralized in modern public life. Many people now seek purpose through ideological alignment, not necessarily because they are shallow, but because ideology offers what traditional frameworks once offered: certainty, community, and a story in which one's life matters. When the self feels unmoored, grand narratives become psychologically attractive.

Yet this attraction carries risk. When meaning is fused to ideology, disagreement becomes existential. The person is no longer defending an opinion; they are defending their source of purpose. This intensifies social conflict and increases inner vigilance, because the mind must continuously monitor threats to its identity.

Meaning becomes brittle because it depends on constant reinforcement and constant opposition.

Modern life therefore faces a strange tension. We have more freedom than ever, but freedom without shared orientation can feel like weight. We can choose almost anything, but choice without grounding produces anxiety. We can design lives, but design becomes exhausting when the designer is also the material being shaped.

This is why meaning as work belongs among the six pressures. It is not an abstract philosophical complaint; it is a daily psychological burden. A person can carry heavy obligations and still be sustained by meaning. A person can carry light obligations and still collapse under emptiness. Meaning is not optional for the human mind. What is optional is whether meaning is supported by shared structures or demanded as a private manufacturing project.

By the end of this chapter, the reader should see why modern life often feels heavy even in comfort. The burden is not only external. It is the internal demand to justify existence, to curate identity, and to locate purpose inside a world that offers infinite options but little guidance about what is worth wanting.

Part II has described six pressures that define the modern load. In the next part of the book, we will step back and examine a crucial fact that makes these pressures harder to address: many of them are not the product of villains. They are the emergent result of incentives, institutions, and environments that no single person controls. To understand the human load fully, we must understand how systems can become oppressive without intending oppression, and how modern life can become heavy without anyone deliberately making it so.

PART III – SYSTEMS THAT WEIGH

CHAPTER 10

Systems Without Malice

One of the most tempting habits of the modern mind is to look for villains. When life feels heavy, the mind wants a face to attach to the weight. It wants a group to blame, an ideology to denounce, a class to curse, or a shadowy intent to expose. Sometimes villains exist, and sometimes cruelty is deliberate. But much of what makes modern life exhausting does not require malice. It requires only systems that are efficient at producing outcomes while indifferent to the human costs of producing them.

This is one of the central reasons the human load is so difficult to address. You cannot negotiate with an atmosphere. You cannot shame an incentive structure. You cannot defeat a feedback loop by calling it immoral. Systems do not feel guilt, and they do not need to hate you in order to pressure you.

A system is simply a set of rules and incentives that channels behavior. When the rules and incentives are aligned with human well-being, the system can feel supportive, even liberating. When they are misaligned, the system can feel oppressive, even if no one intended oppression. This is why modern people often feel trapped without being able to name who is trapping them. The trap is not a person. It is a pattern.

Modernity is full of patterns that produce pressure as a byproduct. The attention economy does not need to want you miserable. It needs only to reward engagement, and engagement is often easiest to harvest through alarm, outrage, novelty, and comparison. A workplace does not need to want you anxious. It needs only to reward responsiveness and measurable output, and those rewards quietly create norms that colonize time and attention. A market does not need to want you insecure. It needs only to compete relentlessly, and relentless competition converts stability into something that must be earned repeatedly.

In each case, the pressure is emergent. It arises from small rational decisions that accumulate into a collective irrationality.

This is why the feeling of being "on call" is so common. No single person may be demanding that you respond instantly. Yet the environment produces the expectation anyway, because the costs of slow response are distributed while the benefits of fast response are rewarded. A person learns to move quickly not because they are commanded to, but because the system quietly punishes slowness, and punishes it in ways that are often subtle enough to be denied.

The same dynamic appears in time compression. Communication technologies did not set out to make people hurried. They set out to make communication faster, and once it became faster the baseline shifted. The system now assumes speed as normal, and anyone operating at a human pace feels as if they are behind. The pressure is not personal. It is structural.

Understanding this structural quality is essential, because misdiagnosis produces the wrong response. If you believe the problem is bad people, you will spend your energy looking for enemies. If you believe the problem is individual weakness, you will spend your energy on self-criticism and private coping. If the problem is systemic misalignment, then neither scapegoating nor self-blame will be sufficient, because the pressure will keep returning.

Systems also have another trait that makes them heavy: they tend to optimize what can be measured. Measurement is not evil. Measurement is often necessary. But measurement narrows attention. What can be counted becomes what matters, and what cannot be counted becomes invisible. Once invisibility sets in, human realities that resist quantification—depth, meaning, calm, trust, wisdom—are treated as luxuries or irrelevancies, even when they are precisely what makes life livable.

This is how metric-driven environments quietly deform human behavior. People start to produce what is measured rather than what is meaningful. They perform for the indicator rather than for the purpose. Over time, the person's inner life begins to align with the system's external demands. Self-worth becomes tethered to output, responsiveness, visibility, and the approval of evaluative mechanisms that cannot see the whole person.

None of this requires malice. It requires only a system that rewards certain behaviors and ignores the costs of rewarding them.

A further complication is that many modern systems are distributed. There is no central authority and no single lever to pull. Platforms, markets, bureaucracies, institutions, and cultural norms interact in ways that produce consequences no one fully controls. A person can therefore feel pressured by a thousand small forces rather than one large force, and this diffusion makes resistance difficult. It is easier to resist a tyrant than to resist a probability distribution.

This is why modern people often experience a peculiar blend of freedom and helplessness. They can choose their city, their job, their identity, their entertainment, their beliefs, and their communities, yet they feel as if life is still running them. The freedom is real, but the environment is structured. A person is free within a maze, and freedom inside a maze still requires constant navigation.

This chapter is not an argument against systems. Civilization is systems. The point is to recognize the difference between systems that serve human ends and systems that consume human attention for their own reinforcement. Once a system becomes self-reinforcing, humans become inputs. They provide data, labor, compliance, and engagement, and the system grows stronger by extracting more of the same.

This extraction can be soft, even pleasant. It can arrive disguised as convenience, entertainment, and opportunity. Yet a system can be gentle and still be draining. The human load increases not only through suffering but through saturation, not only through oppression but through constant subtle demands that never fully resolve.

The most important consequence of "systems without malice" is moral confusion. People sense that life is becoming heavier. They sense that something is wrong. But because the pressure does not have a clear villain, they oscillate between anger and self-blame. They alternate between conspiracy thinking and therapy thinking, between political rage and private coping, and they often end up exhausted by their own attempts to explain their exhaustion.

A clearer diagnosis reduces this confusion. If the weight is structural, then structural responses matter. That does not mean grand revolution. It can mean redesign, boundary restoration, incentive correction, and institutional humility. But none of that becomes possible until we stop mistaking emergent pressure for personal failure or deliberate persecution.

In the next chapter, we will examine one of the most powerful engines of system pressure in modern life: measurement and surveillance, broadly understood. The promise of metrics is clarity. The cost is exposure. As systems become more capable of tracking behavior, performance, and even emotion, the human nervous system begins to live in a new climate—one in which evaluation is not occasional but ambient, and in which privacy is not assumed but negotiated.

CHAPTER 11

Metrics, Surveillance, and Psychological Exposure

Modern societies measure more than any societies in history. Measurement has brought undeniable gains: greater coordination, improved safety, increased efficiency, and the ability to see patterns that were once invisible. Yet measurement also reshapes the inner life. When observation becomes continuous, the human nervous system adapts as if evaluation were constant, even when no judgment is actively being rendered.

This is the core shift this chapter examines. Surveillance today is not only about cameras or databases. It is about living in an environment where behavior, performance, preference, movement, and output are increasingly trackable, recordable, and comparable. The pressure arises not from being watched at every moment, but from knowing that one *could* be watched, scored, or reviewed at any time.

The human mind evolved to respond strongly to social evaluation. Approval and disapproval once came from identifiable people within a bounded group. You knew who was watching, what they valued, and when judgment occurred. Modern evaluation is different. It is often anonymous, delayed, automated, and abstract. The evaluator may be an algorithm, a composite score, a future reviewer, or an invisible audience whose standards are opaque and shifting.

This uncertainty matters. A known judge can be anticipated. An unknown judge cannot. When standards are unclear, the mind compensates by becoming cautious. It over-monitors. It rehearses. It self-censors. The person learns to behave as if they are always potentially on display, because the cost of being unguarded feels higher than the cost of vigilance.

Metrics intensify this effect by translating complex human activity into simplified indicators. Metrics are powerful precisely because they reduce ambiguity. They tell systems what to reward and what to ignore. Yet human lives are not reducible without loss. When metrics become dominant, the parts of life that resist measurement begin to disappear from institutional attention, even though they remain central to human experience.

This creates a subtle distortion. People begin to organize their behavior around what can be counted rather than what matters. They optimize for visibility, responsiveness, and compliance, because those are legible to the system. Qualities such as depth, patience, wisdom, and restraint become harder to justify, not because they lack value, but because they lack metrics.

The psychological consequence is exposure. The self feels increasingly transparent to systems that do not know it personally. A person may not consciously fear surveillance, yet still experience the ambient tension it produces. The nervous system interprets constant measurability as constant risk, because measurement implies judgment, and judgment implies consequence.

This exposure does not need to be punitive to be stressful. Even positive metrics can create pressure. Praise can raise expectations. High scores can become fragile identities. Once a person is known for performance, they feel compelled to maintain it. The system rarely says, "You have done enough." It says, "Continue."

Surveillance also alters time. Records persist. Actions that once vanished now remain searchable, retrievable, and potentially recontextualized. The past becomes less forgiving, because it no longer fades naturally. The mind responds by becoming more careful in the present, knowing that today's behavior may be tomorrow's data. This temporal extension increases self-monitoring and reduces spontaneity.

There is a difference between accountability and exposure. Accountability is relational and contextual. Exposure is ambient and indiscriminate. Modern systems often confuse the two, assuming that more data produces better outcomes. Yet the human cost of constant exposure is rarely counted, because it is diffuse and difficult to quantify.

This cost appears as tension without incident. People feel watched without knowing by whom. They feel evaluated without knowing against what standard. They feel pressure without being able to locate its source. The nervous system remains slightly activated, not because danger is present, but because judgment is possible.

Over time, this climate changes behavior. People become risk-averse in subtle ways. They avoid experimentation, complexity, and nuance, because these do not score well. They simplify themselves to fit categories that systems can process. The self becomes legible at the cost of being whole.

It is important to distinguish this argument from paranoia. The claim is not that someone is always watching you personally. The claim is that environments of pervasive measurement train the mind as if judgment were continuous. This training occurs regardless of intent, and it affects even those who are not targets of scrutiny.

Measurement and surveillance therefore contribute to the human load by creating a persistent sense of exposure. The mind expends energy managing impressions, maintaining consistency, and anticipating interpretation. This energy is rarely acknowledged, because it is not attached to a single task. It is the background cost of living in a measurable world.

The deeper danger is not loss of privacy alone. It is loss of interiority. When every action is potentially externalized, the inner life begins to shrink. Reflection feels risky. Ambivalence feels unsafe. Silence feels suspicious. The person becomes fluent in performance but less comfortable with inwardness.

This inward erosion matters because the inner life is where meaning, judgment, and restraint are formed. A civilization that measures everything but understands little will produce efficient systems and exhausted people. Measurement without wisdom does not eliminate error; it multiplies it by scaling the wrong incentives.

This chapter does not argue for abandoning metrics or rejecting technology. Measurement is indispensable to modern civilization. The argument is about proportionality and humility. Systems must recognize what they can measure well and what they cannot measure at all. When they fail to do so, they externalize their limitations onto human nervous systems.

In the next chapter, we will step back and examine the broader trajectory these systems are creating. The question is no longer whether modern life is heavy. The question is where this weight is leading, and whether civilization is willing to adjust course before the load exceeds what human psychology can sustainably carry.

CHAPTER 12

The Direction of Travel

It is possible to read the previous chapters as a critique of modern life and still miss the central point. The point is not that modernity is uniquely evil, or that technology is a mistake, or that the past was superior. The point is that modern systems have outpaced the human nervous system, and they are still accelerating. The question is not whether the human load exists. The question is whether the load is increasing, and what happens if it continues to increase without redesign.

The direction of travel is toward greater interconnection, greater measurement, greater speed, and greater cognitive dependence on external systems. These trends are not speculative. They are already visible in daily life, and they arise from incentives that reinforce themselves. Interconnection produces coordination, coordination produces efficiency, efficiency produces competition, and competition produces pressure for more interconnection. The system does not require a master plan to keep moving. It moves because movement is rewarded.

This is why the human load is likely to intensify, even if the quality of life improves in many material ways. Material comfort and psychological weight are not the same thing. A person can live longer, safer, healthier, and richer and still feel more strained, because strain is often produced by complexity, evaluation, and incessant demand for attention. Modernity solves old problems and creates new burdens, and the new burdens are often less visible because they do not arrive as hunger or violence. They arrive as saturation.

The most important driver of this saturation is that modern systems are increasingly becoming environments rather than tools. Technology does not merely assist human activity. It structures human activity. It organizes time, attention, social life, economic opportunity, and even the language through which people interpret themselves. As this structuring deepens, human beings become more dependent on systems they do not fully understand. Dependence is not inherently bad, but it changes the psychology of agency. A person may feel capable and yet feel that life is being run by processes outside their control.

The second driver is the expansion of measurement. Measurement spreads because it is useful, and because it can be automated. Once something can be measured cheaply, it tends to be measured continuously. Once it is measured continuously, it becomes legible to systems that reward and punish. Once rewards and punishments become automated, human behavior adapts. The environment becomes more efficient, and the person becomes more exposed.

The third driver is acceleration. As tools remove friction, expectations rise. As expectations rise, people move faster to avoid falling behind. As people move faster, they have less time to reflect, and when reflection decreases, systems face less resistance. The cycle tightens. A fast world therefore tends to become faster, because slowness begins to look like failure rather than restraint.

The fourth driver is the growing role of algorithms in shaping social reality. Algorithms do not merely recommend content. They curate attention, shape social mood, and structure the flow of information in ways that influence belief, identity, and conflict. This influence often operates below conscious awareness, which makes it more powerful. People believe they are choosing when in fact they are being guided, not necessarily toward truth or well-being, but toward engagement and predictability.

As artificial intelligence becomes more capable, these drivers deepen. AI increases speed by automating cognition. It increases measurement by extracting patterns from massive datasets. It increases dependence by providing assistance that becomes difficult to live without. It increases exposure by making human behavior more legible. These are not dystopian fantasies. They are normal consequences of systems becoming more powerful.

Yet this is also the moment where the book must be careful. The point is not to fear these developments reflexively. The point is to see them clearly and to recognize that capability is not the same as alignment. A system can be astonishingly capable and still misaligned with human needs. If civilization treats human attention as extractable, human time as infinitely compressible, and human identity as permanently measurable, then more capable technology will amplify those assumptions.

This is the risk. The human load will grow not because technology becomes evil, but because technology becomes efficient at scaling incentives that already produce strain. Without redesign, the future becomes a more automated version of the present: faster, more measurable, more connected, and more demanding. The burden will be distributed unevenly, but the baseline climate will move toward greater vigilance and less slack.

However, the direction of travel is not destiny. Systems can change. Incentives can be redesigned. Boundaries can be restored. Norms can be reshaped. The same intelligence that built these environments can also build better ones, and the same technology that intensifies load can also reduce it if it is used with humility about human limits.

This chapter therefore functions as a hinge. It shifts the book from diagnosis to orientation. It clarifies that the six pressures are not temporary side effects. They are structural features of a civilization in motion. The question becomes whether modernity will continue to treat human beings as adaptable inputs, or whether it will acknowledge that biological limits are real and that a sustainable civilization must respect them.

In the next chapter, we will make one boundary explicit. The answer is not to go back. It is not to romanticize the past or seek refuge in regression. The only viable path is forward, but forward with design rather than drift. To move forward well, civilization must first reject the fantasy that the past was a better home for the human mind. It was a smaller home, and sometimes smaller feels lighter, but smaller was also harsher. The solution to modern weight is not older life. It is a better future.

PART IV – CARRYING THE FUTURE

CHAPTER 13

Why the Answer Is Not Going Back

When modern life feels heavy, the mind reaches for an obvious remedy: reduce the weight by returning to an earlier world. The impulse is understandable. People are tired of being reachable at all times, tired of constant comparison, tired of endless choice, tired of living inside systems that never fully switch off. They look at the past as a place with fewer demands, fewer inputs, fewer expectations, and therefore fewer pressures. They imagine a slower pace and a calmer mind, and they interpret that calm as evidence that the past was more human.

The intuition has a grain of truth. The past was smaller, and smallness often feels lighter. Yet smallness is not the same as goodness, and lightness is not the same as dignity. The fact that the human nervous system sometimes prefers older conditions does not mean older conditions were a better home for human beings. It means that modern systems have expanded faster than our biology has adapted, and expansion without redesign produces strain.

This chapter closes the door on the fantasy of return, not because the past contains nothing worth admiring, but because returning is neither possible nor desirable. Civilization cannot unknow what it knows, and it cannot uninvent what it has built. Even if a person could personally retreat, the world they retreat from would still exist and still shape the conditions of life around them. The past is not a refuge. It is a memory with edited footage.

The most common form of nostalgia is selective nostalgia. People imagine the parts of earlier life that provided rhythm and coherence—bounded communities, predictable expectations, clear roles, stable calendars. They often forget, or quietly minimize, the price paid for that coherence. Earlier worlds were more rigid. They constrained choice, policed deviation, and often treated people as functions rather than individuals. Many lives were not only hard but short. Many people lived with chronic physical labor, limited mobility, and limited access to medical care that modern people now take for granted without noticing.

The past also locked most people out of knowledge. It did so not through conspiracy but through scarcity. Education was limited, books were rare, institutions were gatekeepers, and expertise was concentrated. This concentration produced a kind of social stability, but it also produced intellectual dependency. Most people had little access to the broader world of ideas, and therefore little ability to question the frameworks they inherited. Some frameworks were wise. Many were not. Yet the person's freedom to revise them was constrained by ignorance as much as by authority.

It is easy to romanticize a world when you forget how easily that world could destroy you. It is easy to admire simplicity when you forget that simplicity often came from exclusion. It is easy to praise slow time when you forget that slow time was frequently filled with unchosen hardship. The past did not feel calm for everyone. It felt calm primarily for those who fit.

Even when older worlds did provide psychological structure, they did not do so in ways compatible with modern moral expectations. They often achieved cohesion through conformity, social enforcement, and limited exit options. The absence of overwhelming choice was not always a gift; it was often a constraint. People did not have to "curate identity" partly because identity was assigned, and assignment came with punishments for deviation. The small village, for all its warmth, was also capable of suffocation.

This is why "going back" is not a solution. It trades one set of pressures for another set of pressures and does so by sacrificing freedoms that are ethically difficult to relinquish once recognized. It also misunderstands the nature of the current problem. The current problem is not that modernity exists. The current problem is that modern systems are misaligned with human limits, and misalignment cannot be corrected by retreat into a world that was aligned only because it was narrower, poorer, and more coercive.

There is also a deeper reason regression is impossible. Human intelligence is not a detachable feature. It expands capacity, but it also expands awareness of alternatives. Once a society becomes conscious of possibilities—medical interventions, broader education, global knowledge, higher living standards, expanded rights—it cannot credibly pretend those possibilities do not exist. The knowledge itself becomes part of the human environment. People can resent that fact, but resentment is not the same as reversal.

Modern movements that promise return often succeed emotionally because they translate complexity into blame. They take the real burdens of modern life and attach them to a single cause: elites, technology, immigration, capitalism, the state, decadence, or some other explanatory villain. The promise is that if the villain is defeated, the earlier simplicity will return. Yet simplicity rarely returns. What returns is conflict, because the world does not become smaller again. It merely becomes harsher.

A healthier stance is to treat nostalgia as data rather than as instruction. The longing for older conditions reveals what human minds need: rhythm, boundaries, belonging, and the feeling that life is comprehensible. Those needs are real. The error is to assume the only way to satisfy them is to resurrect a past that cannot ethically or practically be resurrected. The task of civilization is to build modern structures that provide what older worlds provided psychologically without recreating what older worlds imposed morally. That is not an easy task, but it is the only viable task.

This is why the solution must be forward. It must involve design rather than drift, deliberate boundaries rather than accidental friction, and technologies that serve human ends rather than technologies that harvest human attention. It must involve recognizing that the human nervous system has limits and that those limits do not disappear because machines become faster. If anything, faster machines make those limits more urgent.

A forward solution also requires intellectual honesty about what modernity has already achieved. Modern life is often heavy, but it has also extended human lifespan, reduced many forms of suffering, expanded rights, and democratized access to knowledge. The correct response is not to deny the load or to glorify the past. The correct response is to keep the gains while redesigning the conditions that produce unnecessary strain.

The goal is not a return to simplicity. The goal is a civilization mature enough to handle its own complexity. That maturity begins with a refusal to romanticize regression and a willingness to confront the real question: if we are not going back, what are we going toward, and how do we ensure that what we build is worthy of human beings?

The next chapter answers that question by returning to the most important fact in this entire book. Human beings are not merely overwhelmed animals in need of smaller worlds. They are profoundly sentient creatures, capable of reflection, meaning, and deliberate self-direction. The proper aim of technology, and of civilization itself, is not to shrink human life until it feels manageable. It is to expand human life while making it sustainable.

CHAPTER 14

Sentience, Not Efficiency

Modern debates about technology are haunted by a category error. They assume that the primary question is what machines will do *to* us: whether they will replace our labor, hollow out our institutions, or erode what remains of human relevance. These fears are not frivolous, but they are misdirected. They mistake function for essence. They ask whether machines will outperform humans at tasks, when the deeper question is whether civilization understands what humans are *for*.

Human beings are not distinguished by their ability to produce output. They are distinguished by their capacity for sentience: the ability to experience awareness, reflect on experience, assign meaning, imagine alternatives, and judge between them. This capacity is not incidental. It is the central feature around which every durable human civilization has quietly revolved, even when it has failed to articulate it clearly.

Sentience is not simply intelligence in the narrow sense. It is not computation, recall, or pattern recognition. It is the ability to *inhabit* experience rather than merely process it. A sentient being does not only act; it understands itself acting. It does not only respond; it evaluates the response. It does not only live in time; it reflects on what time is doing to it.

This is what makes humans uniquely capable of wisdom, morality, and long-term responsibility. It is also what makes them uniquely vulnerable to overload.

Modern life strains sentience not because it demands too much labor, but because it demands too much *attention without meaning*. The human mind evolved to engage deeply with a limited number of problems at a time, embedded in contexts where action, consequence, and understanding were closely linked. Contemporary systems break that link. They flood awareness with signals, requests, evaluations, and abstractions that require response but resist resolution.

Technology did not create this strain, but it has intensified it by accelerating the mismatch between capacity and demand. Tools that once extended human reach now define the environment in which human cognition operates. They shape what is visible, what is urgent, what is rewarded, and what is ignored. In doing so, they quietly teach people what kinds of thinking matter and what kinds do not.

The tragedy is that this has happened precisely at the moment when technology could have enabled the opposite outcome.

For most of human history, sentience was a luxury constrained by necessity. Survival demanded constant physical labor, logistical coordination, and attention to immediate threats. Reflection existed, but it was fragile and often confined to elites with time, education, and institutional protection. The majority of human intelligence was spent on maintenance rather than meaning, not because people lacked depth, but because depth was costly in environments that offered little slack.

Advanced technology changes this equation fundamentally. When machines can absorb much of the cognitive and logistical burden that once consumed human life, the opportunity emerges to reallocate attention toward what machines cannot do: interpretation, judgment, ethical reasoning, creativity, and care. In other words, technology creates the conditions for sentience to move from the margins of civilization to its center.

This is why the fear of "replacement" is so revealing. Replaced from what, exactly? From tasks that exist primarily because no better tools once existed? From roles that reward compliance, speed, and repetition rather than understanding? To treat liberation from such labor as an existential threat is to confuse activity with purpose and busyness with worth.

The real danger is not that machines will outperform humans. It is that civilization will continue to organize itself as if performance were the highest human value. In such a world, technology becomes a force multiplier for the wrong priorities. It accelerates output while flattening meaning, increases efficiency while eroding judgment, and scales systems that grow more powerful even as the people within them feel less oriented.

A civilization that prizes efficiency above sentience will inevitably use technology to extract more attention, compress more time, and measure more identity. It will mistake legibility for understanding and responsiveness for wisdom. Human beings in such a system will remain busy, connected, and productive, yet increasingly estranged from the inner capacities that give life coherence and dignity.

The alternative is not technological restraint in the sense of retreat or regression. It is conceptual restraint: a refusal to treat humans as infinitely adaptable inputs and an insistence that technology serve explicitly human ends. Those ends are not mysterious. They include the preservation of interior life, the protection of sustained attention, the cultivation of judgment, and the creation of space in which meaning can form without being immediately monetized, measured, or optimized away.

Technology worthy of human beings must therefore meet a higher bar than usefulness. It must respect the limits of awareness rather than exploit them. It must reduce cognitive noise rather than amplify it. It must support judgment without replacing it and inform decision-making without colonizing the process by which decisions acquire moral weight.

This is not a naïve hope. It is a design challenge. Systems already exist that lighten the human load rather than increase it, not because they are less advanced, but because they are built around an explicit understanding of human limits. The problem is not capability. The problem is intent embedded in structure.

What modern civilization lacks is not intelligence, data, or tools. It lacks a shared agreement about what intelligence is *for*. Until that agreement is made explicit, technology will continue to scale whatever incentives dominate by default, and default incentives rarely favor sentience. They favor speed, visibility, and short-term performance, because those are easiest to reward and easiest to automate.

The future, then, does not hinge on whether machines become more humanlike. It hinges on whether humans insist on remaining fully human in a world of increasingly powerful machines. That insistence requires clarity about what must not be optimized away: reflection, ambiguity, slowness where slowness is necessary, and the capacity to say that not everything valuable can be measured or accelerated.

Human beings do not need smaller lives, simpler tools, or a return to narrower worlds. They need environments that fit their nature: environments that recognize sentience as a fragile achievement rather than a free resource, and that treat awareness not as fuel for systems, but as the point of civilization itself.

If modern technology is guided by that understanding, it will not diminish humanity. It will finally allow humanity to show up fully, not as overextended operators inside indifferent systems, but as sentient agents capable of meaning, responsibility, and deliberate self-direction.

That is the promise worth defending.

That is the future worth building.

CHAPTER 15

Designing for Human Limits

Once sentience is recognized as the central human capacity worth protecting, a number of assumptions that dominate modern life begin to loosen. The question is no longer how much more humans can endure, adapt to, or absorb. The question becomes how systems should be designed if human awareness is treated as finite, fragile, and valuable rather than inexhaustible and free.

This shift in framing matters because most modern systems were built under a different premise. They assume that attention can always be redirected, time can always be compressed, and cognition can always be stretched further without consequence. When strain appears, it is interpreted as an individual failure of resilience rather than a signal of structural misalignment. The system remains unquestioned; the person is asked to adapt. Designing for human limits reverses that logic.

Human limits are not defects to be overcome. They are features that make judgment, meaning, and responsibility possible. A mind that cannot pause cannot evaluate. A mind that cannot disengage cannot choose. A mind that is permanently stimulated cannot distinguish what matters from what merely demands response. Limits are not obstacles to intelligence; they are the conditions under which intelligence becomes usable.

The first implication of this recognition is that not all efficiency gains are neutral. Some efficiencies reduce waste. Others remove friction that served a psychological purpose. When transitions disappear, when pauses are eliminated, and when recovery is treated as latency rather than necessity, systems may become faster while people become less oriented. The loss does not show up immediately, but it accumulates as fatigue, irritability, and a sense of being perpetually behind.

A civilization designed for sentient beings must therefore preserve friction intentionally. This does not mean glorifying slowness or rejecting progress. It means acknowledging that some processes require time not because technology is insufficient, but because understanding is slow by nature. Reflection cannot be rushed without being degraded, and judgment cannot be automated without being distorted.

The second implication is that continuous engagement is not a virtue. Modern environments often reward constant availability, rapid response, and visible busyness. These signals are easy to measure, which is why they dominate institutional logic. Yet they correlate poorly with insight, creativity, or wisdom. In many cases, they actively undermine them. A system that treats uninterrupted attention as idle time will eventually exhaust the very capacities it depends on.

Designing for human limits requires reinstating boundaries that protect interior life. These boundaries can be temporal, spatial, or normative. They may take the form of clear stopping points, periods of disconnection, or cultural expectations that distinguish urgency from importance. What matters is not the specific mechanism, but the acknowledgment that attention must be defended or it will be consumed.

The third implication concerns measurement. Measurement is indispensable to modern coordination, but it becomes corrosive when it expands beyond its proper domain. Not everything that matters can be measured, and not everything that can be measured should be rewarded. When metrics substitute for judgment, systems gain clarity at the expense of understanding. People learn to perform for the indicator rather than for the underlying purpose.

A sentience-centered civilization does not abandon metrics, but it treats them with humility. It recognizes that indicators are maps, not territories, and that excessive reliance on them produces behavior that is legible but shallow. Judgment must retain the authority to override measurement when the two diverge, or else the system will drift toward optimizing appearances rather than outcomes.

The fourth implication is social. Human beings are not solitary processors of information. They are relational creatures whose sense of meaning depends on recognition, trust, and shared norms. Modern systems often scale by anonymizing interaction and abstracting responsibility. This increases efficiency, but it also erodes the relational feedback that helps people calibrate behavior and self-understanding.

Designing for human limits means restoring contexts where responsibility is visible and reciprocal. It means ensuring that people can see the consequences of their actions and understand how their contributions fit into a larger whole. When responsibility becomes diffuse, anxiety rises, because the mind senses obligation without clarity. When responsibility is grounded, effort feels purposeful rather than draining.

None of these principles require rejecting technology. On the contrary, they require more sophisticated use of it. Tools can be built to protect attention rather than fracture it, to reduce noise rather than amplify it, and to support judgment rather than bypass it. The difference lies not in capability, but in priorities made explicit at the design level.

The greatest mistake modern civilization can make is to assume that humans will simply adapt to whatever environments emerge. Adaptation has limits, and adaptation without agency becomes erosion. A system that demands constant adjustment from its people while refusing to adjust itself will eventually hollow out the very capacities that made it successful.

Designing for human limits is therefore not an act of restraint. It is an act of preservation. It acknowledges that sentience is not an infinite resource, but a delicate one, and that a civilization capable of unprecedented power must also be capable of unprecedented care in how it deploys that power.

The future will not be decided by whether technology becomes faster, smarter, or more autonomous. It will be decided by whether systems are designed with a clear understanding of what human beings can sustainably bear. A civilization that learns this lesson can grow without grinding its people down. A civilization that ignores it will continue to scale its own exhaustion.

In the next chapter, we turn to the question of responsibility. If sentience is the point and limits must be respected, then who is accountable for making that alignment real? The answer does not lie with individuals alone. It lies with institutions, designers, and cultures that must decide whether human awareness is something to be protected—or something to be spent.

CHAPTER 16

Automation as Liberation

Modern societies speak about automation as if it were a thief. It is described as a force that "takes" jobs, "replaces" workers, and "hollows out" the human role in the economy. The language is revealing. It assumes that a person's dignity is fused to a set of tasks, and that losing those tasks is a form of diminishment. Yet this assumption deserves interrogation, because it is not timeless. It is a cultural arrangement, and like all arrangements it can be altered.

To ask what automation might take is understandable. A person needs stability. A family needs income. A society needs coordination. But beneath these practical concerns lies a deeper confusion: the belief that human worth is best proven through economic necessity. Modern civilization often treats work not merely as contribution, but as moral standing. People are not simply paid for what they do; they are granted legitimacy by having something to do.

This is why the fear of replacement can feel existential. The worry is not only "How will I live?" It is "Who will I be if I am no longer needed in the way I have been needed?" In a culture that equates usefulness with worth, automation can look like eviction from the moral order.

Yet consider what much modern work actually consists of. It is not the cultivation of wisdom, the exercise of judgment, or the creation of beauty. It is often maintenance, administration, compliance, and repetitive coordination. Large portions of the economy exist to manage the consequences of other parts of the economy, creating layers of activity whose primary function is not meaning but continuity. People spend their days answering, sorting, reporting, tracking, aligning, documenting, scheduling, and updating, often with the persistent feeling that what they are doing is necessary only because the system cannot tolerate stillness.

To name this is not to insult workers. It is to recognize a structural reality. Many people do valuable work under conditions that degrade them, and the degradation is not proof that the work is noble. It is evidence that the system consumes human attention because human attention has been the cheapest fuel available. Automation changes the price of that fuel.

When machines can perform large amounts of routine coordination and pattern-based labor, society faces a choice. It can treat this as a crisis and attempt to re-create busywork to preserve the old moral arrangement, or it can treat it as an opportunity and redirect human effort toward what human beings do uniquely well. The first option is emotionally tempting because it preserves familiar identities. The second option is harder because it requires rethinking what we reward and why.

The most common public failure in this debate is to treat "jobs" as the unit of meaning. Jobs are not meaning. Jobs are arrangements for producing value and distributing resources. A job can be meaningful, but it can also be empty, corrosive, and spiritually deadening. A society that treats job preservation as the highest end risks preserving the very structures that have increased the human load. It risks fighting to keep people stuck in roles that fragment attention and drain inner life, simply because those roles have been culturally interpreted as proof of worth.

Automation therefore threatens not humanity, but a particular ideology of humanity. It threatens the belief that necessity is the only reliable source of discipline and purpose. It threatens the idea that if people are not forced to work, they will collapse into laziness and meaninglessness. That fear is not entirely irrational, because many modern lives have been organized around obligation rather than orientation. If obligation disappears without replacement, some people will indeed feel lost. But that would be an indictment of the culture, not of human nature.

A healthier view is that automation can remove the cognitive rubble that fills so much of modern life and return attention to higher-order human capacities. The most valuable human contributions are not speed and repetition. They are judgment under uncertainty, ethical reasoning, creative synthesis, and care—forms of intelligence that require sentience, context, and meaning. Machines can assist these capacities. They cannot replace them without turning society into a system that operates efficiently while thinking shallowly.

This is why the real risk is not replacement but atrophy. If people outsource judgment, they will lose the habit of judgment. If they outsource memory, they will lose the habit of internal continuity. If they outsource choice, they will lose the practice of moral responsibility. Automation can liberate, but it can also sedate, and sedation is not the same as freedom.

Civilization must therefore draw a distinction between automation that replaces drudgery and automation that replaces agency. The first can lighten the human load. The second can erode the very capacities that make humans worthy of protection. A tool that reduces unnecessary burden is a gift. A tool that encourages human passivity is a quiet threat, even if it feels convenient.

This distinction also clarifies why technological fear is often a failure of imagination. People imagine a world where machines do the work and humans are idle. They rarely imagine a world where machines do the drudgery and humans become more fully human. They rarely imagine a society that treats reflection as a civic virtue, care as a form of contribution, and wisdom as a skill that must be cultivated rather than a luxury for the few.

The problem is that such a society would require cultural maturity. It would require replacing the moral status of busyness with the moral status of responsibility. It would require teaching people to use liberated time not as entertainment alone, but as space for meaning, learning, relationship, and the deep work of becoming a coherent self. Automation makes this possible. It does not make it automatic.

This is why the question is not whether automation will arrive. It is how it will be interpreted. A society that clings to the old equation—worth equals labor, labor equals necessity—will experience automation as humiliation and threat. A society that recognizes sentience as the central human value will experience automation as leverage and release.

The future will contain both tendencies. There will be disruption and there will be opportunity. The decisive factor will be whether civilization understands what it is trying to protect. If it protects only productivity, it will preserve a world of endless maintenance. If it protects the inner life—attention, judgment, meaning—then automation can become one of the most profound civilizational gifts in history: not the replacement of humans, but the restoration of what makes them human.

In the next chapter, we will widen the lens further. Modern technology is not only changing work. It is becoming a form of civilizational immune system—detecting threats, managing complexity, and protecting fragile societies from shocks that would otherwise overwhelm them. The question is whether we can accept these protective powers without allowing them to evolve into forms of control that diminish the very agency they were meant to preserve.

CHAPTER 17

Technology as Civilizational Immune System

Civilization is not a natural state. It is a fragile achievement, maintained against a background of forces that do not care whether human societies endure. Disease, resource shocks, infrastructure failure, conflict, and environmental volatility are not moral events; they are realities. For most of human history, the margin between stability and collapse was thin. The past sometimes felt slower, smaller, and psychologically simpler, but it was also less protected. It was not virtuous. It was exposed.

This is why the modern debate about technology often feels strangely selective. People rightly critique the ways contemporary systems overload attention, compress time, and erode interior life. Yet many of the same people romanticize a world that could not sustain large populations, could not prevent predictable outbreaks, and could not absorb major shocks without severe human cost. The impulse to retreat from modernity often forgets that modernity's heaviest pressures coexist with modernity's strongest protections.

A useful way to see this is to treat advanced technology as a civilizational immune system. An immune system does not exist to make an organism feel comfortable. It exists to keep the organism alive. It detects threats, mobilizes response, and prevents small problems from becoming fatal cascades. Civilizational technology plays a similar role. It monitors conditions, distributes resources, coordinates responses across distance, and maintains the complex infrastructure that makes modern life possible. These functions are largely invisible when they work well, which is why they are easily undervalued.

Consider disease. The most obvious "pressure" of modern life is psychological, but one of the greatest gifts of modernity is biological security. Vaccination, sanitation, antibiotics, diagnostics, and surveillance of outbreaks have transformed the human relationship with pathogens. That transformation did not come from wisdom alone. It came from tools, institutions, and scientific infrastructure powerful enough to detect a threat early and respond at scale. A civilization that rejects these capacities in the name of simplicity does not return to human authenticity. It returns to vulnerability.

The same is true of basic material stability. Modern societies are complex webs of energy, logistics, communications, and coordination. Food supply chains, power grids, water systems, and emergency services operate as continuous background miracles. They are maintained not by nostalgia but by systems engineering, predictive monitoring, and rapid response. When these systems fail, the result is not philosophical discomfort. It is immediate hardship, and it tends to cascade because complexity amplifies breakdown.

Advanced technology also protects civilization from existential risk, a category of threat that earlier eras could not meaningfully address. Climate volatility, pandemics, nuclear escalation, and large-scale cyber disruption are not problems that can be solved by local virtue. They require early detection, strategic coordination, and tools capable of acting at the scale of the threat. A civilization without advanced technological capacity is not morally purer. It is strategically fragile.

This is the point that much anti-modern sentiment misses. A society can be psychologically lighter and still be physically doomed. It can feel human and still be unable to defend itself. The goal is not to choose between comfort and security. The goal is to build security without turning security into domination.

That is where the tension begins, because immune systems can become pathological. An overactive immune system does not merely protect. It attacks the organism it is meant to defend. In civilizational terms, this is the danger of monitoring becoming control. The tools that detect threats can also detect deviations. The tools that coordinate response can also enforce compliance. The systems that manage risk can also manage behavior.

This risk grows as technology becomes more capable. Sensors become ubiquitous, data becomes permanent, and predictive models become persuasive enough to justify intervention. The argument for control always arrives wearing the language of safety. Sometimes the argument is legitimate. Sometimes it is opportunistic. The problem is that once monitoring infrastructure exists, it rarely remains confined to a single purpose. Capabilities seek application, and institutions tend to expand their remit when they can.

The challenge, then, is not whether civilization should have an immune system. It must. The challenge is whether that immune system can be designed with constitutional humility. In biological terms, immunity must be strong enough to detect threats and restrained enough to avoid autoimmunity. In civic terms, technology must be capable enough to prevent collapse and constrained enough to preserve agency and interior life.

This is not a question that can be solved by good intentions alone. It requires design principles that treat human sentience as the protected asset, not as collateral damage. When systems detect risk, they should minimize intrusion. When they coordinate response, they should preserve room for judgment. When they measure behavior, they should distinguish between what is necessary for safety and what is simply convenient for administration. A civilization worthy of sentient beings does not confuse manageability with legitimacy.

This also means acknowledging a reality that many people avoid: advanced civilization without advanced technology is not stable. It is not virtuous. It is precarious. Complexity is not a lifestyle choice that can be reversed by preference. Once a society reaches a certain scale—population, infrastructure, interdependence—its survival depends on systems that can coordinate and protect at that scale. The correct response is therefore not to dismantle capability, but to civilize it.

To civilize technology is to embed it inside a moral frame that is explicit about ends. The ends are not mere prosperity. They are not mere efficiency. They are the preservation of human agency, the protection of interior life, and the reduction of unnecessary load. Technology can defend civilization from external threats while also being redesigned to stop behaving like an internal threat.

This is the bridge into the conclusion. We have named the human load as real and structural. We have rejected withdrawal and regression as fantasies. We have argued that automation and advanced systems can be liberating if they are aligned with sentience rather than with extraction. Now we can state the final requirement clearly: the future must be carried consciously.

In the conclusion that follows, we will gather the book's argument into its simplest form. The task is not to flee modernity. The task is to demand technologies, institutions, and norms worthy of sentient beings. Civilization will continue to grow more powerful. The only question is whether it will grow wise enough to remain human.

CONCLUSION

Carrying the Future Consciously

This book began with a simple claim: the human load is not an individual failure. It is structural. Modern life is heavy not because people have become weaker, but because the environment has changed faster than the nervous system, faster than social norms, and faster than the inherited rhythms that once made life psychologically legible. The result is a chronic condition of partial activation—too much input, too much evaluation, too much choice, and too little resolution.

Seen clearly, this removes a great deal of unnecessary shame. It also removes a great deal of false optimism. You cannot solve a structural problem through private virtue alone, and you cannot meditate your way out of an environment designed to fragment attention, compress time, and treat human awareness as fuel. Individuals can cope, adapt, and protect themselves at the margins, but the deeper weight remains because it is built into systems. The question, then, is not whether a person can become tougher. The question is whether civilization can become wiser.

The second claim followed from the first: the answer is not withdrawal. The fantasy of return is emotionally seductive because it promises relief through reduction, but it confuses smallness with goodness and simplicity with dignity. Earlier worlds were often psychologically bounded, but they were also materially harsher, intellectually narrower, and morally restrictive. Modernity's pressures are real, yet modernity has also expanded safety, knowledge, and opportunity in ways that cannot be unlearned. We do not need to go back. We need to go forward without drifting.

To go forward well requires a reordering of priorities. Modern systems tend to optimize what is measurable: speed, visibility, engagement, responsiveness, productivity. These are not meaningless values, but they are not ultimate values, and when they become supreme they quietly degrade what cannot be easily quantified. Depth becomes a luxury. Wisdom becomes inefficient. Interior life becomes an inconvenience. A civilization that treats attention as extractable, time as infinitely compressible, and identity as permanently measurable will eventually produce people who are outwardly functional and inwardly exhausted.

The alternative is not anti-technology. It is a demand for technology worthy of human sentience. Sentience is the central human fact. It is the ability to inhabit experience, reflect on it, judge it, and orient one's life within it. It is what makes meaning possible, and it is what makes responsibility real. Technology can either expand this capacity or degrade it. It can either protect interiority or colonize it. It can either reduce noise or amplify it. Capability alone does not decide the outcome. Design does, incentives do, and above all the chosen ends do.

This is why the future must be carried consciously. Civilizations rarely collapse because they lack tools. They collapse because their tools scale the wrong incentives, and because their complexity becomes unmanaged. Advanced technology can function as a civilizational immune system, protecting societies from disease, infrastructure failure, and existential shocks that older worlds could not withstand. Yet immune systems can become pathological. Monitoring can become control. Safety can become an excuse for permanent exposure. Coordination can become soft domination. The task is not to abandon the immune system. It is to civilize it.

To civilize it means making explicit what modern life too often leaves implicit: that human beings are not raw material for systems. They are sentient agents. Their attention is not an infinite resource. Their time is not merely a commodity. Their identity is not a dataset. A culture that forgets this will build astonishing machines and steadily diminish the inner life of the people who built them. A culture that remembers it can build machines that lift burdens without eroding agency and that accelerate capability without shrinking meaning.

The practical implication is not a list of personal tips. It is a moral stance: refuse the premise that constant engagement is normal, refuse the assumption that everything valuable must be measurable, and refuse the idea that efficiency is the final judge of what deserves to exist. These refusals do not require romanticism. They require maturity. They require institutions that restore boundaries, designers who treat attention as something to protect, and citizens willing to demand systems that respect human limits rather than testing them for sport.

Modern life will not become lighter by accident. It will become lighter only if civilization decides that human awareness is worth defending. That decision is not abstract. It expresses itself in norms, incentives, and designs that either preserve slack or eliminate it. It expresses itself in whether the default expectation is availability or presence, performance or judgment, exposure or interiority. Every generation inherits a technological world. Only some generations insist on shaping it deliberately.

The human load is real. It is also not final. We are approaching an era in which powerful tools can remove drudgery, widen access to knowledge, protect civilization against threats that once guaranteed collapse, and amplify the best capacities of the reflective mind. The question is whether we will use that power to build a world that treats sentience as the point of the whole enterprise—or whether we will allow the future to be built by default incentives that do not know what a human life is. The future will arrive either way. The only choice is whether it arrives consciously.

FURTHER READING

Attention, Distraction, and the Attention Economy
Carr, Nicholas. *The Shallows.*
Newport, Cal. *Deep Work.*
Hari, Johann. *Stolen Focus.*
Williams, James. *Stand Out of Our Light.*
Zuboff, Shoshana. *The Age of Surveillance Capitalism.*

Stress, Overload, and the Modern Nervous System
Sapolsky, Robert. *Why Zebras Don t Get Ulcers.*
Maté, Gabor. *The Myth of Normal.*
Burkeman, Oliver. *Four Thousand Weeks.*
Kahneman, Daniel. *Thinking, Fast and Slow.*
Schwartz, Barry. *The Paradox of Choice.*

Technology, Measurement, and Surveillance
Muller, Jerry Z. *The Tyranny of Metrics.*
O'Neil, Cathy. *Weapons of Math Destruction.*
Noble, Safiya Umoja. *Algorithms of Oppression.*
Benjamin, Ruha. *Race After Technology.*
Postman, Neil. *Amusing Ourselves to Death.*

Work, Status, and Meaning
Graeber, David. *Bullshit Jobs.*
Sennett, Richard. *The Corrosion of Character.*
de Botton, Alain. *Status Anxiety.*
Frankl, Viktor E. *Man s Search for Meaning.*
Becker, Ernest. *The Denial of Death.*

Modernity, Systems, and the Human Condition
Bauman, Zygmunt. *Liquid Modernity.*
Han, Byung-Chul. *The Burnout Society.*
Rosa, Hartmut. *Social Acceleration.*
Stiglitz, Joseph E. *The Price of Inequality.*
Piketty, Thomas. *Capital in the Twenty-First Century.*

Artificial Intelligence, Automation, and Civilizational Risk

Tegmark, Max. *Life 3.0.*
Bostrom, Nick. *Superintelligence.*
Susskind, Daniel. *A World Without Work.*
Harari, Yuval Noah. *Homo Deus.*
Ord, Toby. *The Precipice.*

www.ingramcontent.com/pod-product-compliance
Lightning Source LLC
LaVergne TN
LVHW090420210926
848480LV00002B/630